D1556565

Corporate Social Responsibility
Case Studies for Management Accountants

Gweneth Norris
University of South Australia

John Innes
University of Dundee

ELSEVIER

AMSTERDAM • BOSTON • HEIDELBERG • LONDON
NEW YORK • OXFORD • PARIS • SAN DIEGO
SAN FRANCISCO • SINGAPORE • SYDNEY • TOKYO

CIMA Publishing is an imprint of Elsevier

CIMA
PUBLISHING

CIMA Publishing
An imprint of Elsevier
Linacre House, Jordan Hill, Oxford OX2 8DP
30 Corporate Drive, Burlington, MA 01803

First published 2005

Permissions may be sought directly from Elsevier's Science and Technology Rights
Department in Oxford, UK: phone: (+44) (0) 1865 843830; fax: (+44) (0) 1865 853333;
e-mail: permissions@elsevier.com. You may also complete your request on-line via
the Elsevier homepage (http://www.elsevier.com), by selecting 'Customer Support' and
then 'Obtaining Permissions'

British Library Cataloguing in Publication Data
A catalogue record for this book is available from the British Library

Library of Congress Cataloguing in Publication Data
A catalogue record for this book is available from the Library of Congress

ISBN   0 7506 6660 9

Typeset by Integra Software Services Pvt. Ltd, Pondicherry, India
www.integra-india.com
Printed and bound in Great Britain

Contents

Acknowledgements

The authors wish to thank the Research Foundation of the Chartered Institute of Management Accountants for funding the research on which this book is based. This research project was developed following discussion with Professor Rob Gray, Director of the Centre for Social and Environmental Accounting Research, and Maria Sillanpaa of the Institute of Social and Ethical AccountAbility. We acknowledge the helpful comments of three anonymous reviewers. We wish to thank Kim Ansell, Kamla Best and Jasmin Harvey of the Chartered Institute of Management Accountants, Mike Cash of Elsevier and all the managers and accountants who gave generously of their time and knowledge in helping us to prepare the four case studies contained in this book. Without their assistance this research project would not have been possible. We dedicate this book to all our interviewees.

Executive Summary

Stakeholder groups and social performance

The four case studies were selected on the basis of their extensive external social reporting. The stakeholder groups identified by the interviewees in the four organisations were similar, namely: communities, customers, employees, environment, shareholders and suppliers. However, in discussions about social performance, interviewees said relatively little about customers (except for customer satisfaction measure) and shareholders. The ranking given to these stakeholder groups varied between the four organisations.

The interviewees considered that their organisation wished to be an ethical organisation respected for its environmental and social performance but the interviewees also suggested that such an image was 'good for business'. The interviewees considered that the increased organisational costs caused in the short term by improved social performance would be more than offset by the long-term benefits for the organisation. For example, all four organisations made use of their social performance image in their marketing. Interviewees considered that good corporate social performance has an ethical perspective but also a self-interest perspective.

Social performance had slightly different meanings for different interviewees but the following common aspects emerged:

1. Community involvement including:
   (a) employees participating in community projects
   (b) educational liaison including employees giving talks in schools, courses for school projects and teacher placements
   (c) community support including sponsorship
   (d) development of disadvantaged communities in developing countries into mainstream suppliers.
2. Environmental aspect including:
   (a) environmental sustainability
   (b) recycling materials
   (c) reduction in energy usage
   (d) environmental management courses for customers.

3. Employees including:
   (a) 'treating employees right'
   (b) how each employee's job fits into the rest of their life
   (c) feedback on managers from their subordinates
   (d) employee morale.
4. Suppliers including:
   (a) ethical trading policy (including paying suppliers on time)
   (b) developing long-term relationships with suppliers
   (c) how suppliers treat their own employees and their own suppliers
   (d) suppliers' environmental impact.

Externally reported social performance measures, social values and decision-making

In three of the four case studies, interviewees generally ignored or even did not know about the externally reported social performance measures. One reason for this was that a small unit (divorced from the operational managers and management accountants in the organisation) reported these social performance measures. Most interviewees considered their organisation's external social report to be a separate event that did not affect their decision-making. In summary, almost all the interviewees considered that externally reported social performance measures had very little direct impact on managerial decision-making.

However, all four organisations had their explicit values such as effect on society, concern for individual, concern for environment, concern about policies of suppliers, management by fact, valuing staff, ethical behaviour, trust and integrity. Two of the four organisations had a specific social values group. All four organisations also showed a willingness to transmit their values to others.

The four case studies include many examples where the social values of the organisation had influenced managerial decision-making. Examples of social values influencing managerial decision-making included the following:

1. design of products and packaging
2. use of recycled materials and refillable containers

3. reduction in use of energy
4. ethical investment
5. not dealing with companies whose ethics and values did not match that organisation's brand values of integrity and trust
6. social inclusion for insurance (i.e. including members of the community previously excluded from insurance) by working with local councils to offer a good value insurance policy linked to the tenants' rent
7. educational liaison activities with schools and staff working on community projects.

Internally and externally reported social performance measures

The general view emerging from the interviewees in the case studies was that the main purpose of externally reported social performance measures was for public relations aimed not only at shareholders but also at the community and customers. Generally the externally reported social performance measures did not come from the internal management reporting system but were collected as a one-off exercise by a self-contained unit (divorced from the operational managers and management accountants in the organisation). As a result, very often there was no internal management reporting, monitoring or management of such externally reported social performance measures. Basically there was no Internal Social Performance Information System (ISPIS) and little Internal Social Performance Information (ISPI) for managers.

One finding was that the internally reported social performance measures were much less developed than the externally reported social performance measures. Indeed in Cases A, B and C there were relatively few internally reported social performance measures, and only in Case D were the internally reported social performance measures linked to those published in the social report. In Cases A, B and C, there were few explicit links between the internally and externally reported social performance measures.

The internally reported social performance measures included the following:

1. In relation to community involvement:
   (a) number of staff secondments
   (b) charitable amount raised by staff
   (c) number of employee hours per week on community projects.
2. In relation to employees:
   (a) employee morale index
   (b) employees' perceptions of job security
   (c) index of job offering feeling of personal accomplishment.
3. In relation to the environment:
   (a) data on CO_2 emissions
   (b) data on water use
   (c) volume of waste produced and amount recycled.
4. In relation to suppliers:
   (a) employees have proper written contracts
   (b) factories have proper licences from the government
   (c) impact on the environment.

Social information needs of managers

Managers generally considered that they received too little social information and, in particular, both accountants and managers agreed that there were too few social performance measures reported internally. Managers suggested that they would like to receive the following information about community involvement:

(a) numbers involved in community initiatives such as work experience, teacher placements and school visits
(b) survey results such as quality of feedback in relation to community involvement
(c) costs and values of community involvement.

In addition managers considered that there were generally too few output or outcome social performance measures. However, perhaps the simplest change is to ensure that there are explicit links between the externally and internally reported social performance measures. Most interviewees believed that such a development and expansion of the internal social performance measures would help managers to act to improve the organisation's social performance.

Social performance measures and performance evaluation system

Social performance was not part of the formal performance evaluation and remuneration system. Almost all the interviewees recognised that if social performance is part of the organisation's mission statement and is an important aspect of its business, then both the performance evaluation and remuneration systems for individuals needed to take a contribution to the organisation's social performance explicitly into account.

Developing internal social performance information systems

The findings of this research project suggest the following ten recommendations for management accountants to consider if they wish to implement internal social performance reporting:

1. Implementation team involving a management accountant and managers led by a manager.
2. Consult managers about the social information and social performance measures required.
3. If your organisation has an external social report, develop explicit links between the externally and internally reported social performance measures.
4. If your organisation does not have an external social report, consider developing first internal social performance measures and reports.
5. Develop logical links between your organisation's mission statement/objectives and your internally reported social performance measures.
6. Develop internal social performance measures for each of your organisation's stakeholder groups.
7. Check that the internally reported social performance measures include both input and outcome measures.

8. Develop a formal system for internal monitoring and management of social performance.
9. Develop explicit links between managerial evaluation (and remuneration) and contribution to organisation's social performance.
10. Remember that the internally reported social performance measures are important but so are the organisation's culture and social values that affect social performance – often through informal employee group control and employee self-control.

External social reporting is important but so is internal management information on social performance. In the final analysis, it is the strategic and operating decisions of managers and other employees that determine the social performance of an organisation.

Introduction

Objectives

This research project explores the internal management information in relation to social performance for four organisations that publish relatively detailed social performance information either in their annual reports or in a separate social report. One objective is to link such published social performance information with the social performance information provided for managers. The decisions of such managers impact on the performance measures reported in these published social reports.

The three main objectives of this research project are to discover

1. The meaning of social performance for accountants and managers and, in particular, the stakeholder groups mentioned by interviewees in relation to social performance.
2. The extent to which externally reported social performance measures influence managerial decisions.
3. In relation to social performance measures
   (a) the degree to which internally and externally reported social performance measures are consistent
   (b) the information needs of managers with respect to the social performance measures
   (c) the links between externally reported social performance measures and the internal performance evaluation system.

Case studies

In the four case studies these three objectives are discussed in the findings section of each case under the headings of stakeholders, decision-making and internal performance measures. The four case studies are large organisations with a reputation for external social reporting. One of the case studies is in the retail sector and three are in the financial services sector.

The two authors have been involved in over 100 case studies but in this research project they experienced a new problem. This was the first time that the authors have had agreement from five different organisations to participate in a research project and then, before the research began, each of these five organisations changed its mind.

Obviously there could be a number of reasons for such a change of mind. Managers are very busy and each of the five organisations may have decided after more consideration that it could not afford the managerial time involved. The change of mind may be due to the way in which the researchers approached the organisation. In previous case studies the authors have usually gained access to organisations via the finance director or management accountant. In this research project the authors approached the person responsible for the external social reporting. In five organisations this person was enthusiastic at first about the research project and gave permission for that organisation to become a case study. However, after speaking to managers within the organisation, this permission was withdrawn. One possibility is that although such organisations were active in their external social reporting, they may have been less active in their internal social reporting. For example, one of the best known organisations for external social reporting was frank enough to admit that 'we have not gone very far down the road of internal reporting of social information and, therefore, would prefer not to be involved in this current research project'. The main point to keep in mind is that the four case studies in this book may not be typical cases. The four case studies may be at the leading edge of internal social reporting.

A grounded theory approach (Strauss and Corbin, 1998) was followed for the case studies. In each case study between 10 and 19 interviews were conducted with at least two accountants and at least eight managers being interviewed in each organisation. The interview time in each case varied between 15 and 30 hours with almost all the interviews being recorded and later transcribed. Notes were also taken during the interviews and copies of various internal and external documents were also obtained. A structured set of detailed coding procedures was used to analyse the data collected. As a result the findings are grounded in the data – particularly the interviewees' comments. A draft case report was given to each organisation for any comments or suggested changes.

Overview

A short literature review is presented in Chapter 2 under the headings of social reporting, social performance, managerial processes, social accountability versus management control and focus on practice. This literature review helped to sensitise the researchers to the area under investigation so that they could ask relevant, but general, questions during the case studies. There were no preconceived propositions but rather the aim was to allow the findings to emerge from the case studies. The findings from these four case studies in Chapters 3 to 6 are grounded in the interviewees' comments. As a result, fairly extensive quotations from the interviewees are given in Chapters 3 to 6. Chapter 7 is a cross-case analysis of the four case studies and is structured on the basis of the three main objectives of this research project. The conclusions are presented in Chapter 8.

Literature Review

Focus on social reporting

Frederick (1994) suggested that there were three periods in terms of social reporting:

1. Corporate social responsibility 1950–1960s
2. Corporate social responsiveness 1970s to mid-1980s
3. Corporate social rectitude mid-1980s onwards.

Gray *et al.* (1995) and Matthews (1997) have reviewed the corporate social reporting literature. The existing social reporting theories such as legitimacy theory, political economy and stakeholder theory all have an external reporting emphasis as do the corporate social performance models such as Carroll (1979), Wartick and Cochran (1985) and Wood (1991).

There is a large literature on social reporting (such as Gray *et al.*, 1988 and 1991; Gray *et al.*, 1995; Gray *et al.*, 1997; Matthews, 1997; Adams *et al.*, 1998; Gonella *et al.*, 1998; McIntosh *et al.*, 1998; Lehman, 1999; Gray, 2000; O'Dwyer, 2001) and environmental reporting (such as Harte and Owen, 1991; Adams *et al.*, 1995; Gray *et al.*, 1995; Bebbington and Thompson, 1996; Owen *et al.*, 1997; Bennett and James, 1999; Gray, 2000).

A recent issue of the European Accounting Review was devoted to environmental and social reporting in Europe. Owen *et al.* (2000) pointed out that companies such as BP and Shell have published substantial stand-alone social reports and that the Institute of Social and Ethical AccountAbility and the New Economics Foundation are promoting a 'quality scoring framework' for external social reporting. Gray (2000) gives a useful overview of both historical and current developments in social and environmental auditing and reporting. In this book, environmental reporting is viewed as a subset of social reporting.

One theme emerging from this renewed interest in social reporting is that of stakeholders in addition to that of shareholders. It is being increasingly recognised that shareholders are only one set of stakeholders in an organisation (see, for example, Clarkson, 1995; Donaldson and Preston, 1995; Griffin and Mahon, 1997; Mitchell *et al.*, 1997; Greening and Turban, 2000). Stakeholders in organisations include customers, employees, society and suppliers as well as shareholders.

The critiques of social reporting, such as Gray *et al.* (1991), have concentrated mainly on external social reporting. With this growth in research on social reporting over recent years, the focus has been overwhelmingly on the external reporting of social measures. In contrast, there has been relatively little research into the internal reporting, internal performance measures, managerial decision-making and control in those organisations that publish social information (Estes, 1992).

Social performance

The idea of corporate social performance was developed from the work of Berle and Means (1932) and Bowen (1953). This emphasised corporate social responsibility (CSR) and the accountability of business to society. In 1972 Votaw claimed that corporate social responsibility had come to mean 'something, but not always the same thing to everybody'. Further attempts to define corporate social responsibility in the 1980s were criticised in the 1990s as retaining ambiguity (Clarkson, 1995).

From this idea of corporate social responsibility developed corporate social responsiveness. Frederick (1994, p. 154) suggested that:

> the literal act of responding or achieving a generally responsive posture is the focus of corporate social responsiveness.

Carroll (1979) had developed the first integrated corporate social performance model including economic, ethical and legal aspects. Carroll's ideas were later developed by Wartick and Cochran (1985) with the additional element of social issues management.

Perhaps the most influential corporate social performance model is that of Wood (1991) who added an action component to this model. Wood (1991, p. 693) defined corporate social performance as:

> a business organisation's configuration of principles of social responsibility, processes of social responsiveness and policies, programmes and observable outcomes as they relate to the firm's societal relationships.

There is a small but growing literature on corporate social performance examining the internal factors driving processes of social responsiveness (see, for example, Clarkson, 1995; Sethi, 1995; Swanson, 1995; Greening and Turban, 2000; Husted, 2000 and Woodward *et al.*, 2001). However, in comparison with the research into external social reporting (including social performance measures), there is relatively little research into internal social reporting (such as Bennett and James, 1998 and UN, 2000 in relation to environmental management accounting).

The literature on environmental management accounting has grown in recent years. For example, Epstein and Roy (1998) show how to integrate environmental impacts into capital investment decisions. The Chartered Institute of Management Accountants (1997) outlined the role of the management accountant in relation to environmental management. Burritt (1998) examined cost allocation as a tool for environmental management accounting. Bennett and James (1998) edited a book giving a useful overview of environmental accounting for management including both current and future trends. The United Nations (2000) provided a helpful review of environmental accounting procedures and principles. Nevertheless, despite such emphasis on environmental management accounting, research studies (such as Burns *et al.*, 1996) have shown that managers react to and are influenced by external reporting. This research project tries to meet the suggestion of Wood (1991) for corporate social performance research to attempt to understand the managerial processes motivating the development of corporate social policies.

Managerial processes

Much of the literature on socially responsive decision-making is from the business ethics area. For example, work environment and organisational factors are variables that appear to influence ethical decision-making (Falkenberg and Herremans, 1995; Verbeke *et al.*, 1996; Singhapakdi *et al.*, 2000). The impact of processes of employee socialisation may influence socially responsive decision-making (Soutar *et al.*, 1994). Managerial control systems can also influence employee socialisation (Gatewood and Carroll, 1991). In addition, managerial control systems influence an organisation's culture and values that affect employees' behaviour (Robin and Reidenbach, 1987).

Formal control systems include organisational mission and objectives, budgets, performance measurements and reward criteria.
Gatewood and Carroll (1991) emphasise the importance of formal
performance measurement systems in influencing ethical decision-
making. However, informal systems are also important influences
on the managerial processes. An informal system has shared beliefs
and values that affect the group behaviour of employees
(Falkenberg and Herremans, 1995) in terms of social performance.
The individual values and goals of employees expressed in terms of
their self-control also form part of the informal control system.

Sharfman *et al.* (2000) suggest that managers' personal values
play an important role in decision-making and in making choices
about social issues. Self-control and social control may also be
interrelated. For instance, organisational culture (a form of social
control) may support particular personal values among employees.
The degree to which employees are involved personally in an
organisation's social performance may influence their social values
(Sharfman *et al.*, 2000).

Social accountability versus management control

Despite the earlier debate in the literature on the meaning of corporate social responsibility and corporate social performance, Gray
(2000, p. 247) claims:

> The significant growth in environmental and social auditing and
> reporting which we have witnessed in the last decade or so has
> been accompanied by a similar growth in confusion over termin-
> ology and, perhaps more pertinently, a confusion over what an
> environmental and/or social report or audit is intended to achieve.
> Such confusion manifests itself in the different (usually implicit)
> objectives behind environmental and social reporting and in a con-
> sequential lack of clarity over what an audit – in the financial
> accounting sense of independent attestation – should be.

After an analysis of the four models created by considering external versus internal preparers of reports for external and internal
users, Gray concludes that there are two broad categories of pur-
poses behind public entities compiling social and environmental
reports for external consumption. First is the management control
purpose, 'designed to support and facilitate the achievement of the

organisation's own objectives. Such accounting would include assessing risk, managing stakeholders, image management, identification of social responsibility, public relations, seeking out opportunities and efficiencies, living by one's values (walk the talk), maintaining legitimacy, avoiding surprises, inclusivity, etc.' This purpose intrinsically puts the organisation first.

The second category of purpose is the accountability, democratic and sustainability purpose that puts society first. This category reports such matters as 'the limits of organisational ability' and demonstrates 'the social and environmental cost of economic success'. Whereas the first perspective typically assumes that the organisation is 'a fundamentally benign creation', Gray states that the second perspective makes no such assumption. This assumption of the benign characteristic of an organisation is fundamental to Gray's argument that social audits are 'about good management and management control' and not about accountability.

In the light of Gray's philosophical argument and conclusion, a focus of this book is the examination of the relationship between corporate social reporting and internally reported social performance measures.

Focus on practice

In a report that compares ethical reporting in Germany and the UK chemical and/or pharmaceutical companies, Adams (1999) found that, in contrast to German companies, in the UK companies studied:

◆ Ethics reports were co-ordinated by the head of the environmental department with little or no involvement of communications or public relations departments (p. 31).
◆ There were few people involved in compiling the report (p. 32).
◆ In practice there was a tendency for responsibility for the health, safety and environmental (HSE) report to rest with one individual (p. 32).

More generally:

◆ Corporate culture 'appeared to influence the process of developing HSE and other ethical reports' but that this needs further research (p. 32).
◆ Reasons for publishing ethical reports include public credibility (p. 42), building the image of the company (p. 34), public

pressure, enhancement of the corporate image and sometimes a sharing, by management, of the public's concern about 'corporate impacts' (p. 33).

◆ There was evidence that accountability is not the motivation for reporting (p. 60).

The key emphasis on image building and credibility in Adams' report supports Starovic (2002) who, reporting to practitioners, points out that reputational risk impacts what can be a company's most significant intangible asset: brand. As a quick response to criticism, the production of a corporate social responsibility report can overlook the purpose of such a report. Starovic illustrates by reference to British American Tobacco's first social report (June 2002) that, although audited, was met by accusations of hypocrisy. Starovic (2002, p. 12) argued that 'reporting should be the visible part of the structure. It should be supported by a robust internal architecture for measuring performance and a decision-making capability that reflects a wider range of concerns.' Similarly, Adams (1999) has interesting findings in relation to the processes of reporting.

The concern of investors and their inability, or unpreparedness, to rely on published ethical reports is evidenced by the demand from 30 investment institutions to the world's 500 largest companies that 'they reveal how they are tackling ethical and environmental issues such as global warming' (Hayward, 2002, p. 14).

There has been disagreement about whether, in Starovic's terms, the visible part of the CSR structure is a cause or a consequence of values-based decision-making imperatives. Dey (1999) conducted an in-depth study of an organisation that moved from being a charitable concern to requiring the generation of profits to remain viable. The study documented the development of a social bookkeeping system (see, for example, Dey, Evans and Gray, 1995). Gray *et al.* (1997, p. 329) suggested that:

> the production of social accounts is assumed to have an information inductance effect on the part of organisational managers that will encourage more ethically desirable forms of activity. However the fulcrum of social accounting employed here is the discharge of organisational accountability.

In contrast, Bennett and James (1999, p. 502) have suggested that 'change always comes from within – get things right internally then these basic values will expand outwardly to the relationship between the company and its stakeholders'. As guidance to practitioners, King (2002) published a ten-point plan for starting a CSR initiative, including policy development, company-wide targets and key performance indicators, and, apparently in support of Bennett and James, *ending* with reporting. A key benefit of the plan is claimed to be 'improved operational and process efficiency'.

Thus, we have disagreement about which is the cart and which is the horse. We also have conflicting views, and gaps in our knowledge, about the information managers in CSR firms get and need, and the relationships, if any, between internal decisions, external reports and internal reports. This research project attempts to begin to fill the gap in our knowledge relating to the decision-making, internal performance measures and social information needs of managers in those organisations that publish extensive social information. Such knowledge is important if practitioners are to meet the demands of their public and this, after all, is what the public presume that CSR is. Rose (2003, p. 5) suggested:

> As CSR becomes increasingly prevalent and functional, it is likely in coming years to be shaped by a focus on the nature of the decision-making process, rather than just the decisions made. More to the point, there would seem to be a burgeoning desire that corporations expand their operational machinery to bring in hitherto non-business issues and ensure business strategies are integrated with the many stakeholder constituencies that serve, and are served by, them. As such, the major issues for corporate responsibility in the coming year will be around the culture in which corporations establish and maintain.

Case Study A

Organisation

A is an international retail company with stores in several countries. A's brand is a household name. It has reorganised to create four regional business units responsible for managing its global retail activities.

Data sources

Nineteen interviews were conducted with three accountants and sixteen managers. The total interview time in A was over 30 hours. All the interviews were recorded and later transcribed. Notes were also taken during the interviews. Copies of various internal and external documents were also obtained from A.

Published social information

A published an audited social report and also included social information in its annual report. A's published mission statement emphasised social and environmental performance as well as the needs of stakeholders such as communities, customers, employees, environment, shareholders and suppliers. There are various sections to this social report including community involvement, customers, employees, environment, shareholders and suppliers. This published social report has a wide range of performance targets and a selection of these is given below.

(a) **Community involvement**

The report states that A wishes to contribute to local, national and international communities in which it trades with a code of conduct to ensure fairness and honesty. A had several community involvement performance targets including the following:

1. conduct annual survey of local opinions in specified areas
2. work with managers to integrate community involvement activities into personal development plans
3. share best practices in local community initiatives in different countries

4. support initiatives such as work experience, teacher placements, school visits and annual community arts event in each market

5. set annual budget for local community regeneration initiatives.

(b) Customers

A had several customer performance targets including the following:

1. provide information to customers on any genetically modified ingredients
2. launch comprehensive set of instore materials explaining A's approach to business, its products and its values
3. ensure that 60 per cent of customers do not take a plastic carrier bag
4. increase the amount of refills of refillable products sold to 5 per cent of customer transactions
5. agree an action plan for ongoing dialogue with customers.

(c) Employees (including managers)

A had many employee performance targets including the following:

1. employ more people from ethnic minority backgrounds
2. achieve the Investors in People certification
3. encourage staff and managers to consider flexible working hours
4. provide more training for managers on their responsibilities for communication
5. increase percentage of women in senior management positions.

(d) Environment

A had some environmental targets including the following:

1. reduce average energy use per shop to x KWH per annum
2. eliminate or compensate for distribution fleet's carbon dioxide emissions through tree planting and other initiatives
3. audit all sites to appropriate standards
4. begin an environmental full cost accounting system
5. reduce export freight going by air to no more than 2.5 per cent of total export freight.

(e) Suppliers

A had several supplier performance targets including the following:

1. improve speed of payment to suppliers
2. double the number of suppliers with a three-star rating or higher under the supplier environmental rating scheme
3. provide special support for smaller suppliers both on business and value-related issues
4. introduce code of conduct to ensure probity at all times
5. develop key performance indicator model to assess the social impact of the trading links.

In summary, *A* published an extensive audited social report with many performance targets.

Findings

This section presents the results of the data collected by interviews and also from various documents. The results are discussed under the headings of stakeholders, decision-making, internal performance measures and social values and controls.

Stakeholders

The stakeholders mentioned by the interviewees were communities, customers, employees, environment, shareholders and suppliers. Almost all the interviewees mentioned communities as a very important stakeholder for *A*. For example, most of the interviewees gave examples of community project work in which they had been personally involved. *A* has a full-time community project liaison manager who coordinates such projects. Each staff member spends up to a maximum of six salaried days on such community assistance projects. Another theme mentioned by most of the interviewees was *A*'s community trade suppliers. One interviewee stated:

> *A* tries to identify potential suppliers in developing countries and to help them to become mainstream suppliers. The basic aim is to help disadvantaged communities in developing countries.

This programme identifies potential suppliers in developing countries and assists the communities to develop their goods so that *A* can purchase such goods. *A* also helps these communities to use the income from such trade to improve the standard of living for the whole community. *A*'s aim is to develop such new suppliers into mainstream suppliers who are not dependent only on *A*. One interviewee explained:

> It was always the intention that community trade suppliers would graduate to become mainstream suppliers. Now some of them are quite well established as suppliers.

A few interviewees mentioned customers as stakeholders and emphasised *A*'s aim of trying to improve service levels to customers. Most interviewees mentioned employees as stakeholders and the general view was that *A* 'tried to treat people right'. *A* conducted surveys of the views of its employees including a relatively recent survey from which an employee satisfaction index was derived. There is also an employee dialogue group and *A* has monthly communications meetings for all its employees.

Almost all the interviewees mentioned the environment as a very important stakeholder for *A*. Recycling was a theme to emerge from the interviews. Several interviewees also mentioned *A*'s aim of trying to be 'environmentally sustainable'. For example, *A*'s distribution fleet used green diesel and natural gas even though this involved extra expense. However, one interviewee did say:

> We're very strong internally in terms of recycling but at present we're not as good at environmental measurement.

A few interviewees mentioned shareholders but more interviewees mentioned suppliers as stakeholders. *A* has an ethical trading policy which includes paying its suppliers on time. In fact suppliers were usually paid ahead of time because cash flow was so critical for many of *A*'s suppliers. Where *A* had to discontinue trading with a particular supplier, *A* made every effort to give ample notice to the supplier.

Being a retailer with specific social values, *A* was concerned about the social performance of its suppliers and monitored its suppliers in four main ways:

1. visits to suppliers' factories
2. social audits of major suppliers by an independent third party

3. supply chain integrity programme
4. suppliers' signed declaration.

Indeed *A* was concerned not only about the social performance of its own suppliers but also of its suppliers' suppliers. *A* was usually unable to monitor directly its suppliers' suppliers and instead *A* relied on a signed declaration from its own suppliers and also the efforts of its own suppliers.

Decision-making

All 19 interviewees mentioned the importance of *A*'s values to its day-to-day decision-making. Moreover the only topic mentioned by all 19 interviewees was the values of the organisation. The values and culture of *A* had remained very much the same since it was established. Most of the interviewees identified the social values of the company as including the following:

1. concern for the company's effect on society
2. concern for the individual
3. concern for the environment
4. community service
5. concern for the policies of suppliers.

However, these values were implemented in *A* not by formal management controls but by individual employees' self-control.

This self-control and the impact of *A*'s values or culture on its decision-making can be seen from the following quotes from eight different interviewees:

1. The company's core values are paramount to everything we do.
2. At each level of this company, people actively practise what they preach.
3. Social and commercial decisions are interlinked.
4. People follow the culture and are culturally motivated.
5. The company has a very high set of principles.
6. It is ingrained in the culture of the business that people would not even think about contravening our social values.
7. There are a significant number of things we do because we believe these to be the right things to do and we don't specifically look at the impact on the bottom line.
8. We, our values and who we are, drive a lot of our activity as well.

Managers were expected to make socially aware decisions. One manager gave examples that illustrated such decisions. First, he tried to use sea freight rather than air freight whenever possible. Secondly, *A* used green diesel from environmentally aware diesel providers even though this cost *A* an additional £50,000 per year.

Other managers expressed similar views about taking *A*'s social values into consideration in their decision-making:

> You are expected to take the social values into account.
> You are given time to do the right thing socially.
> Our social values are at the heart of our decision-making.

One manager had worked for other organisations for many years and explained how it had taken him a few months to adjust to the very different environment within *A* – particularly its socially conscious ways of doing business. However, he said that within three months he was acting on his own initiative making environmentally aware long-term decisions.

Several interviewees emphasised how environmental concerns affected their decision-making such as the design of *A*'s products and also the packaging for *A*'s products. *A* emphasised to all its suppliers the importance of recycling materials and minimising waste. For example, *A* promoted the use of refillable containers both to its suppliers and its customers. *A* encouraged its customers not to use plastic bags. *A* also tried to reduce its use of energy.

An example of *A*'s environmental concern was its use of materials for fitting out its shops. It tried to avoid the use of plastics and, wherever possible, it used recyclable materials. For example, it used old wooden railway sleepers rather than new wood. *A*'s community trade programme in the developing countries also had environmental concerns at its heart. *A* tried to help such communities to develop into mainstream suppliers while, at the same time, preserving their own environments. The effects of *A*'s values on its decision-making are summarised in the following quote from one interviewee:

> The values of the company are so integral to the brand in terms of its reason for being, its purpose, that we understand the need to bring, as we say, the values closer to the operating side of the business.

Internal performance measures

Given the large number of performance targets in A's published social report, it might have been anticipated that A would have a very sophisticated internal social performance measurement and reporting system. However, this was not the case. For example, A did not report internally its performance against its externally reported targets. A's internal social performance measures were much less developed than its external social performance targets. As one interviewee said:

> My perspective is that in the past in this company, social reporting was an event unto itself, and it was important to get all this information out there in voluminous detail but in reality it had very little to do with the business at all.

Nevertheless, although there were relatively few internally reported social performance measures, the interviewees still cared passionately about A's social performance. Although there was a lack of internal social performance measures, the employees' self-control and group control (stemming from the culture and values of A) were the important control measures in relation to A's social performance.

Following the employee survey, A established several formal internal performance measures such as:

1. absence rate
2. sickness rate
3. appraisal completion rate
4. employee satisfaction index.

Similarly for its community trade, A set an internal performance target of £x per year which was double the amount for the previous year. For its community involvement scheme, A set an internal performance target of 100 per cent participation by its employees.

A had recognised that its internal performance measurement system had been relatively weak in relation to its social values. One interviewee said:

> At present there is not a clear link between our mission statement and our internal performance measurement system and we are trying to move towards a more holistic way of looking at performance.

Similarly, top management's remuneration was based solely on financial, rather than social, performance and several interviewees recognised that this needed to change. One interviewee suggested in relation to top management's basis of remuneration:

> I certainly believe that unless the basis of remuneration changes, and we include social performance, then we're not really marrying up performance against our mission, so we're not there yet.

However, in the current year a new, small performance-related reward measure was introduced relating to the level of employee participation in community involvement.

Within *A* the most developed area of internal social performance measurement was in relation to its suppliers. This was the area with the most overlap in relation to the externally reported social performance measures but again, when asked, the interviewees did not know about the supplier-related performance measures published in *A*'s external social report. *A* used the following internally reported performance measures in relation to the employees of its suppliers:

1. reasonable working conditions for employees
2. occupational health and safety guidelines are followed
3. minimum age for employees
4. no prison workers
5. employees have proper written contracts
6. workers are not bonded to the company (for example, by debt)
7. employees are allowed to join a formal trade union or association of their choice
8. employees are paid proper rates of pay and are given at least one day off in seven and holidays
9. employees are paid for overtime worked
10. proper grievance and disciplinary procedures
11. workers are free to leave the company after working due notice
12. factories have proper licences from the government.

Similarly there were detailed performance measures in relation to the impact of suppliers on the environment.

Nevertheless, despite these performance measures in relation to suppliers, an important finding was that although *A* published very detailed social performance targets (covering community involvement, customers, employees, environment and suppliers), there were relatively few internal social performance measures. Without any prompting, almost all the interviewees said that the company needed to improve the social information reported to managers.

Managers had information and several performance measures in relation to suppliers and, to a lesser extent, employees but would like more information about *A*'s community involvement and environmental performance. The managers suggested quantitative measures such as employee hours on community involvement (such as work experience and school visits), recycling performance and energy usage. In addition to such quantitative measures, managers would also like qualitative information such as the results of surveys about the quality or outcome of community involvement (both from *A*'s staff and also from the 'recipients' of such community initiatives). Furthermore, several interviewees suggested that both the remuneration system and the internal performance measurement system needed to be expanded to take the various aspects of *A*'s social performance into account.

Social values and controls

Although the internal performance measures had relatively little impact on *A*'s social performance, *A* did influence its social performance in three other important ways. First, *A*'s values were clearly stated in various documents including its mission statement. Secondly, there was a Values Group which produced a monthly Values Report for *A*'s executive committee. This Values Group is a cross-functional group which highlighted actual or potential problems relating to *A*'s values which required top management's attention. One member of this Values Group stated:

> The Values Report is a mechanism of raising awareness to the Executive Committee. So basically we are the eyes and ears, pointing out these are the things that are bubbling under the surface and need attention.

Thirdly, and most important of all, in relation to *A*'s social performance, was its recruitment and induction process. The recruitment process was critical to maintaining *A*'s values with emphasis being placed on the values of the individual being consistent with *A*'s own values. For example, one interviewee claimed:

> For a recent senior appointment, one candidate had the required skills and probably was the best candidate but that vital piece regarding values and interest in community activities was missing so that person was not appointed.

Another interviewee stated:

> Part of the reason why people work at this company is because they feel they want to because of its values.

Several interviewees suggested that applicants to *A* were self-selecting because before they applied they understood *A*'s basic values. Similarly, *A*'s induction process emphasised its social values including working on a community project within the first six months. These recruitment and induction procedures added a form of group control to individual employees' self-control in relation to *A*'s social performance.

It is always difficult to compare the culture and values of different organisations but several interviewees (without being asked) made comparisons with their former employers. For example, three inter-viewees commented as follows:

> The main difference from my previous employer is that this com-pany is a business that is committed socially and environmentally.

> Here it's the first time that I've learnt about true representation and genuine consultation.

> My previous employer had a very strong ethical face but from the inside it was a very different story. This company has a less strong ethical face than my previous employer but inside this company is much more ethical than my previous employer.

These comments suggest that the interviewees perceived *A* as being relatively highly committed environmentally, ethically and socially.

Conclusions

A published a detailed social report which emphasised its environ-mental and social performance and the needs of stakeholders such as communities, customers, employees, environment, shareholders and suppliers. This social report included a large number of performance targets for each stakeholder group. The interviewees in this case mentioned the same stakeholders as in the published report but emphasised particularly communities, employees, environment and suppliers. For example, interviewees mentioned participating in community projects organised by *A* and also *A*'s community trade where *A* looked for suppliers in developing countries who, in time and with *A*'s assistance, could become mainstream suppliers.

In relation to the environment, interviewees mentioned *A*'s attempt to be environmentally sustainable and its emphasis on recycling and minimising energy usage. *A* had an ethical trading policy in relation to suppliers which included acting ethically and paying suppliers on time. Interviewees mentioned that *A* was concerned about the social performance of its suppliers and also of its suppliers' suppliers. *A* monitored its suppliers' social performance with visits by *A*'s employees to its suppliers' factories, social audits of suppliers by independent third parties, a supply chain integrity programme and signed declarations by its suppliers.

There was a general consensus among the interviewees that *A*'s values influenced its managers' decision-making. *A*'s values included concern for *A*'s effect on society, concern for the individual, concern for the environment, community service and concern for the policies of suppliers. One interviewee suggested that 'our social values are at the heart of our decision-making'. Examples of *A*'s concern for the environment affecting its decision-making included the design of *A*'s products and the associated packaging (using recyclable materials), the encouragement of customers to use refillable containers and the use of second-hand and recyclable materials for fitting out its shops.

A's internal social performance measures were much less developed than its published social performance targets. Generally the interviewees considered the published social report as being a separate event and as one interviewee said 'in reality the published social report had very little to do with the business at all'. However, the interviewees cared passionately about *A*'s social performance. *A*'s internal social performance measures were in the areas of employees, community trade and suppliers (especially how suppliers treated employees and the environmental impact of suppliers). Some interviewees recognised that *A* needed to improve its internal social information and performance measurement system and also to link the remuneration of top management more directly to *A*'s social performance.

A influenced its social performance in three important ways. First, *A*'s mission statement and other documents made clear the company's core social values. Secondly, there was a Values Group that highlighted, in its monthly report, actual or potential social performance problem areas. Thirdly, and most important of all, *A*'s recruitment and induction processes took into account the company's social values. For example, in the recruitment process the values of the successful applicants were consistent with *A*'s social values. Similarly, the induction process emphasised *A*'s social values including its community project work. In summary, three findings from this case were that:

1. detailed, published social performance measures do not imply similarly detailed internal social performance measures
2. the culture and values of a company may be as important as the internal performance measurement system in the area of social performance
3. self-control and informal group control by employees may be as important as formal management controls in the area of social performance.

Practical lessons learned

◆ Performance measures included
   1. Community
      (a) percentage of employees involved in community projects
      (b) annual budget for local community initiatives
      (c) annual survey of local opinions.
   2. Employees
      (a) absence rate
      (b) sickness rate
      (c) employee satisfaction index.
   3. Customers
      (a) ongoing dialogue with customers
      (b) survey of customers.

4. Environment
    (a) reduce average energy usage per shop by x per cent
    (b) eliminate or compensate for distribution fleet's carbon dioxide emissions through tree planting and other initiatives
    (c) reduce export freight going by air to no more than x per cent of total export freight.
5. Suppliers
    (a) improve speed of payment to suppliers
    (b) double number of suppliers with a three-star rating or higher under the supplier environmental rating scheme
    (c) buy £x from suppliers in developing countries.

◆ There was a need to link performance targets in the published social report with social performance measures reported internally to managers. Managers wished more social information (both qualitative and quantitative) to be reported to them.

◆ It was useful to have a Values Group reporting regularly to top management.

◆ The remuneration system needed to take into account aspects of social performance.

◆ The recruitment and induction processes were important for maintaining and developing the organisation's values.

◆ The social values and culture of the organisation had a great influence on decision-making at all levels in the organisation.

Case Study B

Organisation

B is a large organisation in the financial services sector and is in the insurance, investments, pensions and savings markets. B's brand is a household name. It has a group structure with several subsidiaries.

Data sources

Ten interviews were conducted with two accountants and eight managers. The total interview time in B was over 15 hours. All the interviews were recorded and later transcribed. Notes were also taken during the interviews. Copies of various internal and external documents were also obtained from B.

Published social information

B did not publish a separate social report but included certain information in its annual report. At the time of the research interviews, B was actively considering expanding the amount of social information that it published externally. The report emphasises the importance of stakeholders such as customers, employees, environment and suppliers. However, a distinctive feature of B is its emphasis on communities and particularly local communities with its community involvement and educational liaison activities.

The mission of B includes the following statement:

> We will aim for excellence by providing quality products, a level of financial security and performance and a quality of service which fully meets the needs of our customers, while at all times being ethical and compliant and maintaining the financial strength of the Group.

The report also emphasises B's brand values of being 'trusted, financially secure and customer driven'. Acting ethically and being trusted are two important themes in B's report.

One aspect of B is its ethical funds and there is a lot of information about the operation of such funds in its report. B has an Ethical Committee chaired by B's Company Secretary and comprising investors in B's ethical funds and also certain senior staff involved in managing the ethical funds. This Ethical Committee meets at least four times a year. It has various functions including the following:

1. ensuring *B*'s ethical policy continues to reflect the concerns of investors in the ethical funds
2. ensuring the processes supporting the ethical policy are robust
3. ensuring *B*'s ethical policy is applied correctly
4. ensuring that *B*'s process for ethical investment is observed
5. discussing voting policy with *B*'s corporate governance team
6. reviewing quarterly investment and marketing reports
7. commissioning market and customer research on ethical issues.

The ethical funds are invested according to negative and positive criteria set out in the ethical policy. Readers of this report are invited to write for a copy of a booklet that details *B*'s ethical policy. The ethical fund favours investment in companies that meet the positive criteria and does not invest in companies that fail the negative criteria. In one particular year 72 per cent of the ethical funds, on average, was made up of preferred companies.

The report details specific companies held by the Ethical Funds that became unacceptable. The report also details the voting record at shareholder meetings. For example, in one particular year the Funds voted against or deliberately abstained on 20 occasions and the companies involved are listed in the report. Reasons for such votes against or abstentions included executive remuneration, adverse impacts on local communities and political donations.

The Ethical Funds conduct an annual survey of investors and over the last three years an average of 40 per cent of investors each year have replied to this survey. *B*'s report states:

> This level of response is extremely high for such an exercise and it demonstrates the interest the Fund's investors take in ethical issues.

B also has a Consumer Panel of ethical investors and uses this Panel to investigate investors' concerns on certain issues more deeply. Such recent research has included genetically modified organisms, greenhouse gases, health and safety issues, human rights and political donations.

Findings

This section presents the results of the data collected by interviews and also from various documents. The results are discussed under the headings of stakeholders, decision-making and organisational values, internal performance measures, community investment and educational liaison.

Stakeholders

The stakeholders mentioned by the interviewees were the community (and particularly the local community), customers, employees, environment and suppliers. Interviewees placed a great deal of emphasis on the customers. It was in the early 1990s that *B* developed its Total Customer Satisfaction strategy with three main operating principles:

1. **Customers** – customers' needs and expectations drive *B*'s actions
2. **Process** – *B* will deliver value through processes which it will seek continuously to improve
3. **People** – *B* will train and develop all staff to realise their full potential to serve our customers.

Every employee attended either a two-day training course or a four-day training course (for senior managers) to reinforce what the practical implications of Total Customer Satisfaction were. One interviewee summed up the changes arising from this Total Customer Satisfaction initiative:

> The very same people who were telling us in the 1980s that we were arrogant, remote, uncaring, subsequently in the 1990s rated us the best company to deal with four years on the trot. Now they say that we're very caring, bend over backwards to help, have simplified our processes, turn things around much more quickly and feel that we're on the customers' side. The culture of the organisation has changed to put the customers first.

Another stakeholder group mentioned by almost all the interviewees was the 'employees'. In some cases this was linked to the service given to customers. For example, one interviewee argued:

> Staff morale is very important. We're very aware that customers are being dealt with by people and if these people are unhappy then they will give their customers a bad experience. That's particularly true on the telephone.

In fact *B* monitors its staff morale index. The purpose of *B*'s HR strategy is

> To create an environment which maximises the contribution and potential of our people towards achieving our business strategy, and enables maximum HR added value.

Recently *B* was awarded the HR Excellence Award for best 'HR Strategy Fit to Business Strategy'.

The recruitment process is viewed as extremely important by *B*. One interviewee described the recruitment process as 'very laborious' and involved:

> several psychometric profiles, interviews, aptitude tests, visits and interviews.

Several interviewees mentioned that *B* tries to measure ethics and values of interviewees. One interviewee said:

> We wouldn't recruit somebody, for example, with low responsibility because we know they wouldn't fit in with the company, because this is a company that expects people to be highly responsible.

B has an annual staff opinion survey and also runs a 'reverse feedback programme' where it is just feedback upwards through the organisation. In addition to finding out why staff are leaving with exit interviews, *B* also surveys staff to find out why people intend to stay. *B* has defined about 90 competencies such as leadership, people management, people development and customer focus. One interviewee commented:

> I think that they're a good organisation to work for and they treat their employees very well.

This was typical of the comments from interviewees.

Several interviewees commented on the paternalistic aspect of *B* but this was changing as exemplified by the following comment from an interviewee:

> There's been a paternalistic streak in the way we manage people in *B* but we are slowly getting rid of the worst aspects of that.

This trend is supported by the following comment from another interviewee:

> There's a culture of supporting, developing and empowering people and the culture within my work area is very much one of encouraging people to use their initiative, to get on and do things and to challenge the status quo.

A number of interviewees appreciated *B*'s range of working patterns and working hours that were particularly helpful for working parents. *B* recognises employees' service after one year, five years and then every five years with small presents. The overall view of the interviewees was summed up by one comment:

> Having worked elsewhere. *B* is certainly the fairest employer I've ever worked for.

A few interviewees commented on environmental aspects such as recycling and reducing energy consumption but the community investment theme (discussed later) was much more significant in *B* than the environmental theme. Similarly, two interviewees mentioned suppliers and being fair to suppliers such as paying on time. There is a preferred supplier list and the expectation of *B* is for long-term relationships with its suppliers. However the interviewees recognised community (especially local communities), customers and employees as by far the most significant stakeholders for *B*.

Decision-making and organisational values

A major theme to emerge from this case was the influence of organisational values on decision-making. This theme was mentioned by almost all the interviewees. One interviewee stated:

> We have values, we have our core values written down, we have them documented at the highest level by our senior executives and that is our doctrine.

Another interviewee expanded:

> One of our core values is integrity and another one of those is valuing staff and a third is management by fact. If you put these three together it defines quite a distinctive leadership style. It's characterised by being caring towards the people that work for you; it's characterised by not working off hearsay or speculation but being able to manage by fact. In other words it's being able to back up decisions with facts, real evidence. It's being able to point to specific things rather than making a decision upon a whim. The integrity theme is something that runs very deep, because it's actually about a culture of openness and honesty.

This value of integrity had become more explicit within *B* during the 1990s but several interviewees considered that integrity had always been the major organisational value. For example, one interviewee said:

> I think what underpins *B* is integrity. It's certainly one of the values that we introduced back in the early 1990s. I say introduced, that's probably not fair. I think *B* was a company that traded on integrity and what it did was to actually bring it more sharply into focus. Integrity sets the tone for all decision-making within the organisation.

Indeed there are specific references in *B*'s group mission statement to being an ethical company. Another interviewee argued:

> In the 1980s and 90s we started to use management consultancy language to describe our values; but, you know, they've been the unwritten values of the organisation for generations.

In *B*'s vision statement there are three brand values, namely

1. financially secure
2. trustworthy
3. caring.

One interviewee referred to the second and third of these brand values as being 'highly ethical values to have'. Another interviewee suggested:

> *B* does business in a very ethical way. We look after our customers, try to give them good service and value for money. We treat people well, whether that be our customers, staff or supplies.

We pay our bills on time. We're a caring company. We care about how we treat our customers. I mean if there's a dispute about whether we are going to pay out on a policy or not, we would normally pay unless we really think we're being ripped off. *B* is caring and ethical and tries to treat all people decently in its decision-making.

Another example in the ethical area is the Ethical Committee that ensures the integrity of the ethical investment funds. *B* has a detailed list of the business and personal competences of Committee members including

1. understanding of the broad range of ethical products
2. understanding of the framework for stock selection
3. awareness of ethical issues
4. understanding of the ethical criteria governing *B*'s ethical funds
5. high level of integrity
6. ability to ask questions to satisfy themselves that the process for ethical investment is being followed
7. ability to be objective in undertaking the supervision of the process for ethical investment.

B has detailed criteria to meet its ethical policy and these include both positive and negative criteria. The positive criteria include investment in companies which

1. make a positive contribution to the environment
2. promote sound employment practice
3. promote products and services which benefit the environment or human life
4. follow good corporate governance practice.

The negative criteria prohibit investment in companies and include companies which

1. damage and pollute the environment
2. test products on animals
3. use intensive farming methods
4. produce or distribute pornographic material
5. produce or sell weapons
6. produce alcohol
7. produce tobacco
8. are involved in gambling.

Internal performance measures

B has a performance measurement scorecard with four sections:

1. customer satisfaction
2. people satisfaction
3. impact on society
4. business results (conventional financial results)

based on the UK/European Quality Award Framework, with the enabling criteria being

1. leadership
2. people
3. policy and strategy
4. partnership and resources
5. processes.

B has detailed performance targets for its four scorecard sections. For example, customer satisfaction targets include an overall measure, and customers' perceptions of *B*'s reliability, empathy and responsiveness. The people satisfaction targets include an overall staff morale measure and employees' perceptions of job security, the job offering a feeling of personal accomplishment and competitive salary. The impact on society comprises basically qualitative measures including

(a) press coverage
(b) extent to which *B* enforces corporate governance in companies where *B* is a shareholder
(c) external recognition awards.

However, two aspects of *B*'s impact on society mentioned by a number of interviewees were community investment and educational liaison programmes. These two aspects of *B*'s impact on society will be discussed separately because the interviewees emphasised their importance for *B*.

Community investment

B has won a number of awards for its work with community projects. The Community Investment Department has four full-time staff who coordinate *B*'s work in five priority areas:

1. health
2. education
3. homelessness
4. older people
5. local environment.

One interviewee stated:

> We try to put something back into the communities in which *B* operates. We do not normally write cheques to charities or bodies that we support. We prefer to support them indirectly – either with staff time or by making *B*'s other resources available to appropriate organisations.

One example of community investment was a staff member being seconded to a charity for three months to improve the charity's administrative system. At any one time at least 15 of *B*'s staff are seconded on such community work for an average period of three months each. One interviewee pointed out the advantages to *B* itself of such staff secondments:

> What we get is a more developed member of staff when they come back to *B*, so we see this as an alternative method of training staff and developing staff talents. We would also like to get some kind of branding opportunity as well, if that is possible.

Another example of community investment is that *B* designs and prints leaflets for charities that would feature *B*'s logo. In addition *B* sponsors promotional videos for charities and has a charity fund. In the 18 months before data collection for this case study began, staff raised over £1 million and *B* itself matched the sum raised. *B* also gives in kind. For example, more than 500 charities and voluntary organisations have benefited in some way from donations ranging from furniture to personal computers. In addition *B* will give staff an hour a week off for volunteering to help with charitable work. Groups of employees often go together and do something for a day or a week in a charitable organisation. Again *B* itself benefits from such team-building exercises.

'Pathfinders' is another example of community investment. In this programme *B* annually offers six homeless young people initial six-month contracts with a view to becoming permanent employees. To date the vast majority have become permanent employees of *B* and others have gone into full-time education. As one interviewee explained:

> How do you select the best manager for those young people? How do you select the best department for these people? How do you coach and counsel managers and how do you coach and counsel the homeless people?

B works with charitable organisations with specialist knowledge of homelessness. *B* assists these new recruits, as one interviewee explained:

> As soon as they get a job, their benefit stops, and normally we pay monthly, so we pay them weekly at first and then fortnightly and then monthly. The next problem is they don't have any suitable work clothes, so we need to sort that out as well.

B is a member of the London Benchmarking group that benchmarks both the cost and value of community investment by different organisations. For example, for *B* the value to each charity of each three-month secondment was an average of over £30,000. *B* believes that healthy communities are a better place to do business and is a member of Business in the Community that supports organisations in becoming involved with community projects. One aspect of Business in the Community is Business Support Groups and *B* has a number of employees involved in such groups. Closely linked to this community investment is *B*'s educational liaison.

Educational liaison

B has three full-time staff who coordinate *B*'s educational liaison initiatives. For example, over 250 of *B*'s staff go into schools and as part of the curriculum do two-hour sessions in schools. Last year 7,000 pupils from 45 schools participated in this project. One interviewee explained:

> We have a programme at the moment which is a video which has three parts to it and we talk round each part of this video. The three parts inform school pupils how to write a CV, how to present yourself in an interview and what work is about. What we're trying to do is make it easier for school pupils to bridge the gap between school and work. We don't go in there saying come and work for *B* or buy *B*'s policies. We go in there because we think it's a good

idea to help school pupils bridge that gap more easily. Yes, we get staff development out of it and the video has *B*'s brand on it but the main thing is, we are trying to help people become more useful citizens faster than they might otherwise do.

Another interviewee was involved in a community school. She helps to promote lifelong learning, good health and well-being not just for the pupils at the school and their families but also for the whole local community. One recent initiative was to start breakfast clubs to feed the children before school. Another initiative was to give pupils better access to computers. The aim is to get the local community involved.

B also sponsors two-day courses involving 500 pupils from 20 schools with 25 of *B*'s staff acting as facilitators for groups of 16 to 17 year olds in business topics. In addition *B* was involved in skills workshops where 1,500 students from over 20 schools and 15 universities learned more about teamworking, problem solving and communicating. *B* has 35 staff mentoring school pupils on a one-to-one basis and there were also 10 teacher placements in *B* in the last year where teachers gain an insight into the organisation and develop their own business and management skills. In summary, *B* has a number of educational initiatives with several hundreds of its staff involved in these initiatives.

Conclusions

The interviewees recognised the community (especially the local community), customers, employees, environment and suppliers as stakeholders. *B*'s employee recruitment process is very thorough with psychometric profiles, interviews, aptitude tests, visits and interviews. During the recruitment process, emphasis is placed on the ethics and values of interviewees. *B* pays a lot of attention to its staff morale index, staff opinion survey and reverse staff feedback. The interviewees recognised *B* as a very fair employer.

One of the most important findings of this case study is the influence of organisational values on *B*'s decision-making. *B* has several core values including integrity and management by fact. A theme emerging from almost all the interviews was the ethical nature of *B* that was viewed also by customers and employees as trustworthy and caring. Another aspect of the ethical nature of *B* is its ethical funds monitored by an Ethical Committee. However, the most important aspect of the ethical nature of *B* is its effect on decision-making.

B has performance measures in relation to customer satisfaction, people satisfaction and its impact on society. One important feature of *B*'s impact on society was its community investment including staff secondments to charitable and voluntary organisations, gifts-in-kind to over 500 charities and jobs for homeless young people. A second important feature of *B*'s impact on society is its educational liaison with hundreds of staff involved in talking to school pupils, running skills workshops, sponsoring courses and mentoring school pupils. The basic objective is to help pupils to become more useful citizens than they might otherwise be.

In summary, *B*'s external reporting of its social accountability was relatively limited with the emphasis on its ethical funds. However, its organisational values such as integrity have had a major influence on *B*'s decision-making. There were some performance measures that influenced decision-making within *B* (such as staff morale index and customer satisfaction) but the most important influence was the culture within *B*. Again the stated values of *B* were important and mentioned by most interviewees. Similarly the time-consuming recruitment process for new employees was another factor affecting *B*'s culture. Nevertheless, it became apparent from most of the interviews that the informal control system and self-control were at least as important as the formal control system in shaping the culture within *B*.

The performance measures in relation to *B*'s impact on society were almost non-existent relative to its performance measures in its other three areas of customer satisfaction, people satisfaction and business results. Despite this, its community investment and educational liaison initiatives were important aspects of *B*'s impact on society. Furthermore, *B* was just beginning to develop its performance measures in this area of its impact on society including both financial (costs and value to society) and non-financial (number of staff involved in such projects). However, it was *B*'s culture rather than its performance measures that was driving developments in this area of its impact on society.

Practical lessons learned

◆ Performance measures included
1. Employees
   (a) staff morale index
   (b) 'reverse feedback programme', i.e. feedback from employees about their managers.
2. Customers: customer satisfaction index
3. Operation of ethical funds: annual survey of investors on ethical issues
4. Community
   (a) number of employees seconded to community projects
   (b) number of employee hours on community projects
   (c) budget in kind (such as computers and furniture for charities)
   (d) number of homeless young people given contracts and number that became permanent employees.
5. Educational liaison
   (a) sponsor a certain number of business courses involving a a certain number of school pupils with some of *B*'s staff acting as facilitators
   (b) run a certain number of skills workshops for a certain number of students on teamwork, problem solving and communicating.
◆ Used the ethical nature of the organisation as a brand value.
◆ Organisational values such as integrity, valuing staff and management by fact were important for managerial decision-making.
◆ Recruitment, induction and training processes were critical for maintaining and developing organisation's values.
◆ Was a member of a group of organisations that benchmarked both the cost and value of community involvement.
◆ Self-control by employees was at least as important as formal control system in influencing the culture and decision-making in the organisation.

Case Study C

Organisation

C is a large international organisation in the financial services sector. It has been established for many years and is in the insurance, investments, pensions and savings markets. Its brand is a household name.

Data sources

Ten interviews were conducted with two accountants and eight managers. The total interview time in C was over 15 hours. Most of the interviews were recorded and later transcribed. Notes were also taken during the interviews. Copies of various internal and external documents were also obtained from C.

Published social information

C incorporates fairly extensive social information into its annual report. For example, it includes the following statement on business ethics and standard of conduct:

> The Group recognises its responsibilities to all those with whom its business brings it into contact, including customers, employees, shareholders, suppliers and the community. It therefore operates a Standards of Business Conduct Policy which provides guidance for every employee to act with integrity in all its business relationships.

C includes a corporate social responsibility statement in its published annual report. This corporate social responsibility statement covers various stakeholders including the community, customers, employees, environment and suppliers. There are also sections on health and safety and human rights. However, this corporate social responsibility statement emphasises two aspects namely supporting communities and environmental activity.

In terms of supporting communities, C includes all its worldwide sponsorships that total over £10 million per year. Of this, over £5 million per year is spent on community activities and charitable causes. C gives examples including funds raised by the staff for a charity chosen by the staff with C matching the funds raised by staff.

The greatest emphasis in *C*'s corporate social responsibility statement is on its environmental activities. This is not surprising given that *C* states that it transformed its environmental programme into a corporate social responsibility programme. *C* has published an Environmental Report. *C* adopted a Group Environmental Policy in 1998 and its environmental programme started in 1999 with progress being reviewed by the Group Board of Directors. *C* contributes to the United Nations Environment Programme for the Insurance Industry and Business in the Environment initiatives.

C also has contributed to a Department of Trade and Industry project to develop environmental accreditation for smaller- and medium-sized businesses. *C* has been involved in a number of other environmental initiatives including leading the development, by a group of insurers and banks, of guidance on environmental management and reporting for the financial services sector. An interviewee explained:

> The aim is to provide a simple route-map for financial services companies to manage and report on their environmental performance in a standard and transparent fashion.

In relation to its own environmental activities *B* states in its annual report:

> The Group's programme aims to integrate environmental considerations into corporate policy, business decision-making, product development and purchasing and supply chain management.

Findings

This section presents the results of the data collected by interviews and also from various documents. The results are discussed under the headings of stakeholders, decision-making, internal performance measures and environmental activities.

Stakeholders

The stakeholders mentioned by the interviewees were the community, customers, employees, environment, shareholders and suppliers. Several interviewees commented on *C*'s support for communities.

Some community support was linked to *C*'s line of business. One aim of *C*'s community effort was to reduce the level of crime and to improve safety. However, some of *C*'s sponsorship activities were unconnected to its line of business such as sponsorship that encourages young people to become involved in conservation projects. One interviewee gave another example:

> Each year the staff select a charity and raise funds for that charity and *C* matches the funds raised by staff.

Some interviewees talked about the customers. For example, *C* had developed a new management information customer database and a new web-based business. One interviewee stated:

> We're going to provide the customers with a lot of financial information to allow them to make an informed decision. Hopefully, they will decide to buy *C*'s products; but, you know, that's all part of the service.

C operated customer relationship management but rather than just sell *C*'s products, it wished to ensure that customers had full information to make an informed decision about which products to purchase. Historically, *C* had an emphasis on products rather than customers but as one interviewee said:

> We realised that we can have a very profitable product but a very unprofitable customer.

Another interviewee said:

> I don't know how to say this, but a lot of it is to do with making sure the advice customers are given is actually customer needs-based advice rather than just selling them the product that we've got to sell them. This is in my opinion one aspect of social responsibility.

Several interviewees mentioned employees as stakeholders in terms of *C*'s social accountability and a particular theme to emerge from the interviewees was teamwork. For example, one interviewee stated:

> I have to make sure that my team works effectively. So I see that as having a social dimension to it. Certainly, it's something I consider when I'm recruiting. Are they going to fit in and are they able to communicate.

One interviewee mentioned 'strong relationships within the team' and another said:

> My own team is meeting at the moment but the session I'm doing this afternoon is part of a group development programme. So, last year for example, I spent quite a bit of time at Wharton University in Philadelphia and I was then working in Malaysia and Singapore and London on group programmes and group development, and through that you're meeting people from all parts of the global organisation. It's giving one a broader perspective as well as encouraging personal relationships, and the programme I'm on is designed specifically to create a global sharing.

A further interviewee explained:

> The whole ethos has been cascaded through the organisation about how important it is to build personal relationships that create better knowledge sharing.

C placed emphasis on employees understanding what their long-term aspirations are and how their job fits into the rest of their life. Interviewees gave a number of examples about how C has managed individual cases. These examples included the use of flexible working hours, reducing the workload of a father whose unborn baby had a heart defect and moving an individual with problems to another more suitable job within C. Employee training was another theme that emerged from the interviews.

The most common theme to emerge from the interviews was the importance placed by C on the environment. Several interviewees commented on the dramatic reduction in the use of paper in C. For example, the staff handbook is now distributed electronically and C's internal website is used as the main channel of communication with staff. Similarly, an increasing percentage of C's customers now used the phone and internet, which did not require either paper policies or paper claim forms. Where paper documents were involved, C now used centralised scanning to reduce the need for multiple copies of documents. Most suppliers' invoices were also now received and paid electronically and there was a plan to expand this electronic method to various types of claims. In addition to reducing its use of paper, C had also reduced its use of energy.

One interviewee explained *C*'s approach to its environmental image:

> We monitor the media carefully to assess the image we have –
> particularly our environmental and social image. We have strict
> environmental controls both for our own organisation and for our
> suppliers. We've got a guy on the United Nations environmental
> programme and there are environmental statements on the wall
> out there.

Another interviewee said:

> I feel personally if this company was doing things that I felt
> were unsound socially or environmentally then I wouldn't work
> for them.

C sponsors awards that encourage initiatives at local authority
level to promote best environmental practice within the business
community.

C also has policies to reduce the need for car travel and to encourage homeworking. An increasing number of *C*'s employees were
now working from home and this had reduced the amount of travel
to and from the office. *C* also offered accredited training courses
(varying in length from one to three weeks) in environmental management to its corporate customers. All *C*'s consulting employees
have completed such courses and they provide environmental consultancy reviews for *C*'s clients. However, interviewees commented
that such social responsibility was not just altruistic but it also
made good business sense.

Interviewees mentioned shareholders in terms of giving them
value and growing their returns. *C* had a specific objective of
producing a normalised after tax real return on equity capital of
a certain percentage over a full underwriting cycle. However, *C*'s
interviewees did not view the shareholders as the dominant
stakeholders.

The interviewees placed a great deal of emphasis on suppliers as
stakeholders. It was much more than just paying suppliers on
time. Several interviewees talked about *C*'s supply chain strategy
including 'persuading policy holders to buy into the benefits of
the supply chain'. This supply chain strategy will be discussed
further in the following section on decision-making.

Decision-making

One of the major impacts of *C*'s environmental and social policies was in relation to its supply chain decision-making. *C* has a list of preferred suppliers who do work for *C*, particularly in relation to claims. Examples of these suppliers include builders, electricians, joiners and plumbers. As part of its tender process, *C* requires potential suppliers to provide a statement of their environmental policy. One interviewee explained the importance of supply chain management in relation to *C*'s environmental impact:

> Our supply chain is critical for us because we've got suppliers who are disposing of salvage and fluids. Also our suppliers use all sorts of things in the repair process and our supply chain team write that into the contracts, not just the obvious contracts, that are the motor and salvage ones, but also the building contracts. For example, if a factory has just suffered a major fire, the way in which materials are disposed of is important.

Another aspect of the supply chain management where environmental considerations had influenced decision-making was the introduction of 'remote vehicle inspections' using modern technology by *C*'s engineers. *C* had a policy of reducing travel by car and in the past *C*'s engineers had always visited garages before repairs to vehicles could be authorised. This involved a very high car mileage by *C*'s engineers. One interviewee stated:

> This year we became the UK's leading user of remote vehicle inspections involving hundreds of repairers. The environmental case for remote vehicle inspections was as important as the financial case.

Environmental factors had certainly influenced *C*'s decision-making in the area of its supply chain management.

Environmental and ethical factors had also influenced *C*'s decision-making in relation to its corporate customers. One interviewee stated:

> It's an explicit statement within our business plan that we'll not deal with companies whose ethics and values don't match our brand values of integrity and trust. Part of it is because we want to be good corporate citizens and part of it is because it makes financial sense. We're spending millions to develop our brand and we don't want it damaged by one deal in association with someone who's dodgy.

There are strict contract signing controls in place to ensure that *C* is happy with any new corporate customer before any contract is signed. In addition, every existing corporate customer contract is being reviewed at present.

Environmental considerations had also influenced *C*'s decision to have all its engineers, investigators and in-house adjusters working from home and using laptop computers. The two main environmental benefits from this decision were a dramatic reduction in the number of journeys to and from the office and a great reduction in the need for paper files and reports. Another decision influenced by environmental considerations was that of developing a company-wide intranet site for claims. This intranet site included support and guidance material and encouraged the sharing of best practice. Again this intranet claims site had led to a reduction in the production and distribution of paper guides.

One more example of *C*'s decision-making being influenced by its view of its social responsibilities was its work in relation to 'social exclusion' (i.e. certain members of the community being excluded from insurance cover). In an attempt to reduce the number of individuals being excluded from insurance cover, *C* has developed arrangements (with approximately 50 per cent of UK councils with a tenant scheme) to offer 'Insured with Rent' contents insurance. *C* was also working with its personal customers providing low cost smoke alarms and driver training programmes because:

> The more that we can reduce the risk, the less we pay out in claims and the less we pay out in claims, the less customers have to pay in premiums, so there is a real interest for the whole industry to actually reduce the risk. The key thing that actually runs through all of this is that there is both a moral element to it and a financial one.

Generally the interviewees considered that *C*'s environmental and social policies were driven by two main factors:

1. it made good financial sense to have such policies (i.e. customers expected it)
2. *C* wished to behave in an ethically and socially responsible manner.

Several interviewees mentioned *C*'s brand values of integrity and trust as being consistent with its environmental and social policies.

The expansion of *C*'s ethical funds was given as another example in this area. Overall, the interviewees had no doubt that *C*'s environmental and social policies had a direct impact on *C*'s decision-making.

Internal performance measures

C operates a balanced scorecard approach to reporting internal performance measurement. The four main areas covered are

1. financial
2. customers
3. internal processes
4. growth and learning.

The financial measures were fairly standard. The customer measures included an overall customer satisfaction index from various customer surveys. *C* also examined customer renewal rates categorised into those with claims during the past year and those with no claim. *C* expected those with claims to have a higher renewal rate than those without claims implying that customers were satisfied with their claim experience with *C*, thus increasing their loyalty to *C*. This is important for *C* because attracting new customers is about five times more expensive than retaining existing customers. The balanced scorecard's customer focus also incorporates the results of surveys about customers' experiences with *C*'s claims system.

C has many internal process measures including efficiency, environmental (see following section), and productivity measures. However, these internal process measures include a number that relate to employees such as the absenteeism rate, staff retention rate and a staff enthusiasm index (derived from surveys of employees). One interviewee explained:

> There are surveys in terms of are we the best place to work and how do people feel about their workplace and everything that goes around that including morale and motivation.

Although these are internal performance measures, many of them (including some relating to employees) are benchmarked externally against other organisations, not only in the same sector but also against other organisations in local environments where *C* operates. This local benchmarking is significant because, as one interviewee explained, 'understanding the availability of skills is quite important in each of our locations'.

C's growth and learning performance measures are mostly related to its employees. For example, *C* attempts to measure its knowledge management and also the development of its employees' skills base. There is a great deal of analysis of the effects of *C*'s training on the development of its employees' skills. However, the growth and learning performance measures within *C* do cover areas other than employees such as IT development and development of *C*'s product range.

To illustrate the measures used, one part of *C* used the following performance measures:

1. Customers
   (a) number of customer agreements
   (b) values alignment (between customers and *C*)
   (c) level of compliance training
   (d) degree of e-commerce implementation
   (e) customer satisfaction index.
2. Internal processes
   (a) level of success of authority audits
   (b) use of e-mail to reduce paper usage
   (c) process improvements
   (d) value from service providers
   (e) employee enthusiasm index.
3. Growth and learning
   (a) knowledge management
   (b) development of teamwork
   (c) IT platform migration
   (d) training and skills developed
   (e) level of development of teamwork programme
   (f) morale and motivation index.

Environmental activities

A major theme to emerge from most of the interviews was the emphasis placed by *C* on its environmental responsibilities. *C*'s contribution to the United Nations and the Department of Trade and Industry environmental initiatives has already been mentioned.

Similarly, *C*'s policies to encourage reductions in both employees' car travel and its use of paper have also been discussed. These policies promoted the increased use of homeworking, 'remote vehicle inspections' by *C*'s engineers and electronic communication. In addition, *C* requires potential suppliers to provide a statement of their environmental policy during the tender process.

One interviewee stated:

> Environmental management is part of our wider responsibility to the community and we are continually trying to improve our environmental performance. We take environmental issues into account in the management of our properties such as the use of natural resources, energy consumption and the treatment of waste. We review our environmental performance against specific targets.

Another interviewee confirmed:

> We take environmental considerations into account in the development and management of our property portfolio. We aim to ensure that our own buildings and our investment properties have good environmental performance such as minimising energy consumption.

In relation to the environmental and ethical performance of *C*, one interviewee explained:

> We are in the portfolios of several ethical funds managed by other companies and we ensure that we fit the investment criteria for our own ethical funds.

Another interviewee said:

> Environmental considerations are integrated into our investment and decision-making processes. Our employees are aware of our environmental management approach and we give them appropriate training.

C's environmental policy is implemented through a series of objectives and targets (such as use of paper, energy consumption and total car mileage) and this environmental policy is reviewed annually. As previously mentioned, *C* not only offers environmental management courses for its corporate customers but also provides environmental consultancy reviews for such customers.

Conclusions

The interviewees in *C* recognised the main stakeholders as the community, customers, employees, environment, shareholders and suppliers. *C*'s support for the community included both charitable donations and support for organisations linked to *C*'s business. *C* also tried to reduce 'social exclusion' by having arrangements with 50 per cent of UK Councils for a scheme promoting 'insured with rent contents insurance'.

C operates a customer relationship management system and tries to ensure that customers have full information and good advice. *C* is very aware of its brand values of integrity and trust and, as a result, will not do business with certain corporate customers with different values from *C*. In relation to employees, *C* emphasises teamwork, training and good personal relationships that create better knowledge sharing.

The main theme to emerge from the interviews was the emphasis given to the environment. When asked why *C* was so interested in the environment, the interviewees were clear that:

1. it made good financial sense
2. *C* wished to behave in an ethically and socially responsible way.

C has reduced its use of paper, its energy usage and its employees' car travel. Environmental considerations are taken into account in the development and management of its own and investment properties. *C* also requires potential suppliers to provide a statement of their environmental policy during the tender process. *C*'s supply chain strategy is an important element of its environmental policy including salvage, repair work (such as disposal of fluids) and demolition of buildings.

C has environmental performance targets and uses a balanced scorecard approach with performance measures for customers (such as customer satisfaction index), internal processes (such as staff retention rate and staff enthusiasm index) and growth and learning (such as growth in employees' skills, development of knowledge management and effectiveness of training). In summary, *C*'s environmental policies have had a significant impact on its decision-making such as its development and management of investment properties, expansion of its remote vehicle inspection system and development of its supply chain.

Practical lessons learned

◆ Performance measures included
1. Employees
   (a) absenteeism rate
   (b) staff retention rate
   (c) staff enthusiasm index (derived from survey of employees).
2. Customers
   (a) customer satisfaction index derived from survey of customers
   (b) customer renewal rates
   (c) number of customer agreements.
3. Suppliers
   (a) pay suppliers on time
   (b) ensure all actual and potential suppliers provide a statement of their environmental policy.
4. Community
   (a) charitable donations
   (b) level of community activities.
5. Environment
   (a) number of employees working from home
   (b) number of car miles travelled by engineers
   (c) paper usage
   (d) energy consumption.

◆ Some of the above performance measures were benchmarked against other organisations both in the same sector and in the local environments where this organisation operated.

◆ This organisation did not do business with certain corporate customers with values that might affect this organisation's brand values of integrity and trust.

◆ There was an emphasis on teamwork, training and good personal relationships that created better knowledge sharing.

◆ Developed guidance on environmental management and reporting.

◆ Tried to integrate environmental considerations into its decision-making processes.

Case Study D

Organisation

D is a large organisation in the financial services sector. It has been established for many years and is in the insurance, investments, pensions and savings markets. Its brand is a household name. *D* has a very flat organisational structure with short lines of communication.

Data sources

Eleven interviews were conducted with two accountants and nine managers. The total interview time in *D* was over 20 hours. All the interviews were recorded and later transcribed. Notes were also taken during the interviews. Copies of various internal and external documents were also obtained from *D*.

Published social information

D published a social accountability report. This report adopted a stakeholder approach with the stakeholders identified as community, customers, employees and environment. *D* aims 'to be an active and responsible member of the community and to consider environmental and social issues in our business planning'.

D also states in its social report that it is committed to serving the interests of its customers. Furthermore, *D* aims 'to ensure that employees have opportunities to contribute to the growth of the business and to achieve personal fulfilment and development'. In addition, *D* is 'committed to upholding best practice and good corporate governance and we aim to work actively with those in which we invest to promote good corporate governance and business practices, take up customer concerns, where appropriate, with those in which we invest and apply high standards to our own business management and governance'.

In a survey of public attitudes related to their social accountability programme, *D* found that over 90 per cent of those surveyed 'agreed that companies have a duty towards society . . . Those surveyed thought the key areas of accountability were environmental impacts, treatment of complaints and equal opportunities. Half those interviewed valued a commitment to responsible investing provided they still received a good return.'

In its social accountability report, *D* published the results of a survey on customer satisfaction and another survey on its image. The social accountability report also has a range of key performance indicators such as to

1. pay 90 per cent of home insurance claims within 48 hours of receipt of the required documents
2. acknowledge written complaints within five working days
3. answer 90 per cent of telephone calls within 30 seconds
4. issue unit trust certificates, savings accounts and bonds within specified time periods
5. have above average persistency (or retention) rate (relative to the industry average) for pensions business
6. have various value for money measures
7. meet training days target per employee
8. retain Investor in People status
9. monitor staff on ethnic origin and gender to ensure compliance with equal opportunities policy
10. benchmark energy consumption and CO_2 emissions against relevant guidelines.

The social accountability report has sections on

1. Social inclusion in financial services (i.e. not excluding any group in society from financial services)
2. Employees
    (a) equal opportunities
    (b) age and service profile
    (c) trade union recognition
    (d) salaries, conditions and benefits
    (e) communications
    (f) training and development.
3. Environment
4. Community involvement
5. Charitable support
6. Corporate governance
7. Survey of companies in which *D* invests
    (a) employee and supplier policies
    (b) consumer issues
    (c) environmental and social aspects.

In summary, *D*'s social accountability report is relatively comprehensive with a lot of detail including key performance indicators. This report also includes an independent review, an independent process review and an independent audit report. Given this external social accountability report, what are the performance measures and social information used by managers within the organisation?

Findings

Social accountability has a relatively short lifespan in *D*, so it was possible to explore the reasons for its development. One such reason was the fact that *D*'s parent organisation 'has gone down the social accountability role'. Secondly, it was 'a response to customer and other stakeholders' concerns over our investment policy'. Thirdly, there was 'the development of *D*'s brand and in particular a realisation that our traditional customer base was changing'. Fourthly, *D* accepts that there are a number of different stakeholder groups but 'those stakeholder groups sometimes have conflicting priorities and *D* considers that a stakeholder approach to social accountability may help to resolve such conflicts'.

This section presents the results of the data collected by interviews and also from various documents. The results are discussed under the headings of stakeholders, decision-making, internal performance measures and Social Values Working Group.

Stakeholders

A theme that emerged from most of the interviews was that of the stakeholder approach. However, different interviewees placed different emphasis on different stakeholders including:

1. customers
2. employees
3. investees (companies in which *D* holds shares)
4. suppliers
5. communities (including *D*'s own neighbours)
6. environment.

Generally the emphasis placed on different stakeholders depended on both the seniority and the job function of the interviewees. The more senior interviewees tended to consider a wider range of stakeholder groups. Not surprisingly interviewees in marketing tended to concentrate on customers and interviewees in personnel tended to concentrate on employees. In short social accountability in *D* did mean different things to different interviewees.

However, all the interviewees were aware of the relatively recent introduction of *D*'s social accountability programme. This programme included involvement with other organisations such as Business in the Community, a benchmarking group, Institute of Social Accounting, various universities, KPMG and various pension funds. *D* had also undertaken 'more dialogue and research with certain stakeholder groups'. For example, customers had been surveyed about their expectations as regards service but also about possible conflicts. As one interviewee said:

> If you say to customers:
>
> 1. *D* should always give the maximum return to customers
> 2. *D* should have an ethical investment policy.
>
> Are those two statements mutually reconcilable, and if they're not reconcilable, which way do the customers shade.

A questionnaire survey had also been conducted of more than half of all staff covering employee satisfaction, employee commitment and links with productivity and even profitability. Another interviewee mentioned:

> We have a major piece of work actually ongoing at the moment with the first set of results from dialogue with our investees (companies that we hold shares in). We identify best practice and then engage with those organisations that don't quite come up to that standard and find out what practical things they're doing to address concerns.

D has a policy of prompt payment of suppliers' invoices but is now also asking its suppliers:

1. how they are dealing with their environmental impacts
2. how they treat their employees
3. how they treat their own suppliers.

D is also concerned about its own environmental impact such as energy consumption and transport. For example, D has negotiated discounts on various forms of public transport, gives interest-free loans for public transport season tickets and operates a car-sharing scheme for employees. In addition to setting energy consumption and CO_2 emission targets, D also encourages recycling such as paper and toner cartridges.

There is a community involvement programme including:

1. cash donations to charities
2. mentoring of teachers
3. employees devoting time to local projects.

D has identified three priorities in the community involvement area:

1. medical charities
2. initiatives that strengthen communities
3. positive development of young people.

However, one interviewee identified how community involvement had changed:

> Community involvement is a whole world away from what we did in the past. Donations are merely one aspect of community involvement. Community involvement is much more self-interested than charitable giving. Community involvement needs to be strategic and needs to support the commercial aims of the business but I believe that it is nevertheless extremely benevolent, but it's no longer philanthropic in a completely detached way.

Such community involvement was considered to make good business sense and, although community involvement meant increased organisational costs in the short run, the interviewees believed that the long-term effects for D of its community involvement would be very positive for its business.

Decision-making

To date the social accountability programme had a limited influence on managers' decision-making although this may be because of its relatively recent introduction. For example, a senior manager stated:

> My perception is that basic accountability has not permeated into the daily decision-making yet. I think at a senior level with *D*, it has, and I think that's manifested in things that we were talking about before, such as our social responsibility investment policy, our environmental policy and one or two other things.

Another interviewee agreed:

> I think social accountability influences decision-making but only at the highest level and at board level down through senior management.

Despite the above comments from two interviewees, there were a few examples of the social accountability programme influencing decision-making. One such example was the justification of the investment in an electronic document management system including:

(a) better service to customers
(b) significant reduction in storage space with overall environmental benefits including less energy usage.

Another example was the new customer relationship management project leading to improved customer service.

However, perhaps the most interesting example was in relation to environmental decision-making and the property committee. One interviewee said:

> I thought it was much better if we integrate environmental decision-making within our normal business decision-making and the place where we make the decisions about property is the property committee so we simply extended its remit, and so far it seems to be working very well.

There is now an environmental management group and their decision-making has affected both *D*'s investment properties (i.e. properties which *D* holds as investments and leases to other users) and *D*'s own properties (i.e. properties which *D* itself uses). One example given was in terms of 'recycling a building'. An interviewee explained:

> We were about to sell an investment property building which was about to be knocked down. However, because we're expanding and operating from more and more sites, we decided that it would be

better for a whole number of reasons, including environment, to have one other building apart from our current one, and it would be much easier to operate from two large buildings than from one large one and a number of smaller ones. So, we are refurbishing this building that was going to be knocked down and we've saved a lot of energy by reusing it although this decision has actually increased our costs in the short term.

Nevertheless, despite the above examples, the general consensus of the interviewees was that to date the social accountability programme had relatively little direct influence on decision-making. In contrast the social accountability programme had more indirect influence on decision-making via its effects on the performance measurement system.

Internal performance measures

The general consensus among the interviewees was that the social accountability programme had influenced *D*'s internal performance measures. However, it was not completely clear cut because some parts of *D* had used performance measures (now key performance indicators) for a number of years. For example, one interviewee suggested:

> Key performance indicators – it's really the non-life claims such as acknowledging new claims, issuing payments, visiting policy holders and we've done that for a number of years and equally for a number of years we've operated a self-audit procedure for regional claims office administration and we've had a number of standards there.

For a number of interviewees the changes to the internal performance measures, following the introduction of the social accountability programme, included better documentation of performance measures, more focused approach to performance measurement and changing attitude in some departments. One interviewee summed it up as follows:

> Since social accountability came along and a need to have key performance indicators, I think it's focused us better. We've now got clear targets to which we need to work towards, so I've seen a change in attitude from various departments and managers. We've all become more focused with a clear sense of purpose which we possibly didn't have two years ago.

Another interviewee expressed a similar sentiment:

> We've had a performance culture in operation for a number of
> years in this Department . . . but we have formalised more and
> more the performance management system.

The internal performance measures are linked to the performance
measures in the published social report. Some of the interviewees
recognised that their internal performance measures placed too much
emphasis on input measures and too little on outcome measures. The
frequency of the internal reporting of these performance measures
varied from weekly to monthly to six monthly. The internal audit
department also audited the information on the internal performance
measures to ensure its accuracy. Some of these internal performance
measures were also benchmarked against other organisations.

A detailed environmental programme with objectives and targets had
been issued. Similarly objectives had been set for the second cycle of
the social accountability programme using 'a traffic lights system of
colour coding' to indicate progress against these objectives, namely

red   = objective is unlikely to be achieved this year
amber = objective will be partially achieved
green = objective on target
blue   = objective achieved.

These objectives were grouped under the following headings:

1. general objectives (3)
2. customers (27 objectives)
3. staff (26 objectives)
4. environment grouped under four headings:
    (a) compliance (3 objectives)
    (b) measure (5 objectives)
    (c) minimisation and conservation (21 objectives)
    (d) communicate and influence (12 objectives)
5. community (10 objectives)
6. investees (11 objectives)
7. others (9 objectives).

In summary D had a very detailed internal performance measurement
system for its social accountability programme. There was also an
internal monitoring system to determine how D was performing

against its detailed objectives. However, one feature was that *D* did not yet have a link between its social accountability performance management system and the formal assessment of the performance of individual employees. This may be because the social accountability programme is still relatively new. A number of interviewees suggested that this lack of integration of the social accountability programme with the formal performance assessment system for individual employees was a weakness that might be corrected in the future.

Social Values Working Group

An important feature of *D's* social accountability programme was its Social Values Working Group. As one interviewee said:

> I make no bones about it, this Social Values Working Group is going to make a difference to this organisation.

This Social Values Working Group drives the social accountability programme and publishes an internal newsletter to keep all employees informed. Facilitators are also used. One interviewee described the role of the facilitators as follows:

> Their role is to pass on information on certain subjects when the Social Values Working Group decides – for example, the facilitators give talks on the environment, disability and various topics.

The interviewees considered the facilitators to be the most important channel of communication about the social accountability programme.

There are about 60 facilitators throughout the organisation including one in each regional office. One interviewee expressed the opinion that:

> The facilitators give an alternative communication medium to the normal management communication system, and we find that there's a good flow of communication, both to the facilitators and back from the facilitators on the social accountability programme.

An interviewee who is a facilitator mentioned the equal opportunities programme as one area where the social accountability programme has made employees more aware of the implications of *D's* equal opportunities programme and one interviewee considered that it had changed *D*'s recruitment policy.

Another area where a number of interviewees saw the Social Values Working Group as making a difference was that of community involvement. The aim is:

> To promote the health and well-being of the communities in which our customers and employees live and work.

However one interviewee complained in relation to community involvement that:

> We haven't yet had systematic stakeholder dialogue, which is a bit of a disappointment to me, because it's certainly something which needs to take place next year.

Furthermore, some community involvement has developed from initiatives in the marketing department. For example, *D* has organised, in association with various football clubs, soccer schools for young people around the country. As one interviewee said:

> We do this entirely of our own accord, and really the only kind of direct payback that we get from it is the sense of goodwill that is engendered in the communities where we've organised these things.

Conclusions

D has introduced its social accountability programme relatively recently. All the interviewees were aware of this programme and the system of using facilitators meant that a two-way communication process had been established. However, despite this, the social accountability programme meant different things to different interviewees. This depended partly on the seniority of each individual within *D* and partly on the functional specialisation of each individual.

D had already begun a stakeholder dialogue with customers, staff and suppliers but had not yet started a dialogue with communities about its community involvement. The main stakeholders recognised by *D* were

◆ customers
◆ employees
◆ investees (companies in which *D* held shares)

◆ suppliers
◆ communities (including *D*'s own neighbours)
◆ environment.

In relation to the environment *D* encouraged recycling and tried to minimise its energy usage. *D* also had an environmental management programme both for its own properties and also for its investment properties that it leased to others. *D*'s policy of encouraging public transport and, if necessary, car sharing had affected most interviewees.

Most interviewees thought that the social accountability programme had influenced *D*'s internal performance measurement system with:

1. better documentation on performance measures
2. more focused approach to performance measurement
3. changing attitudes to performance measurement in some departments.

Generally the interviewees considered that *D* had too much emphasis on input measures and too few outcome measures. *D* had an internal reporting and monitoring system in relation to its performance measures. In addition the internal auditors checked the information produced by the performance measurement system. One weakness identified by some interviewees was the lack of a formal link between the social accountability performance measurement system and the assessment of the performance of individual employees.

Nevertheless, the overall view of the interviewees was that the social accountability programme had influenced *D*'s internal reporting and management. The Social Values Working Group and the facilitators had impacted on areas such as the environment, equal opportunities programme and community involvement. There was a link between *D*'s published social report and its internal performance reporting.

Practical lessons learned

◆ Performance measures included
   1. Community
      (a) donations to charities
      (b) employee time devoted to local projects.

2. Environment
   (a) recycling targets
   (b) targets for carbon dioxide emissions
   (c) energy consumption targets.
3. Customers
   (a) customer satisfaction
   (b) survey of customers about their expectations.
4. Employees
   (a) employee satisfaction
   (b) employee commitment.
5. Suppliers
   (a) pay suppliers on time
   (b) suppliers' impact on the environment
   (c) how suppliers treat their employees
   (d) how suppliers treat their own suppliers.
6. Investees (companies in which shares are held)
   (a) investees' impact on the environment
   (b) how investees treat their employees and suppliers.

◆ Social accountability was developed for several reasons including:
   (a) response to concerns of stakeholders
   (b) resolution of conflicts between stakeholders
   (c) development of brand
   (d) positive for business in the long run although increased organisational costs in the short run.

◆ Internal performance measures were linked to the performance measures in the published social report and were also bench-marked against other organisations.

◆ Environmental management group had affected decision-making including property decisions.

◆ It was recognised that social performance measures placed too much emphasis on input measures and too little on outcome measures.

◆ No link had yet been established between the social accountability performance management system and the formal assessment of the performance of individual employees.

◆ The Social Values Working Group drove the social accountability programme and used 60 facilitators (and an internal newsletter) to keep all employees informed about topics such as community involvement.

7

Cross-case Analysis

This chapter is a cross-case analysis of the four case studies and is structured on the basis of the three main objectives of this research project, namely to discover

1. (a) the stakeholder groups mentioned by interviewees in relation to social performance and
    (b) the meaning of social performance for accountants and managers.
2. The extent to which externally reported social performance measures influence managerial decisions.
3. In relation to social performance measures
    (a) the degree to which internally reported and externally reported social performance measures are consistent
    (b) the information needs of managers with respect to the social performance measures
    (c) the links between externally reported social performance measures and the internal performance evaluation system.

Stakeholder groups

The interviewees both within each case and across the four case studies had a general consensus about the main stakeholder groups in terms of social performance, namely

1. Community
2. Customers
3. Employees
4. Environment
5. Shareholders
6. Suppliers.

In addition, a few interviewees (for example, in Cases A and D) also mentioned the investees (i.e. the companies in which *D* invested) as being another stakeholder group. However, although the interviewees in all four case studies mentioned customers and shareholders in their groups of stakeholders, when interviewees discussed social performance in more detail, relatively little was generally said about customers (except for customer satisfaction) and shareholders. Social performance was discussed much more in relation to community, employees, environment and suppliers. Furthermore, the emphasis given to community, employees, environment and suppliers varied across the four case studies.

Meaning of social performance

Even within the same case study, interviewees emphasised different aspects of social performance. Similarly, although there were significant consistencies between the four cases in their interpretation of social performance, there were also differences. In terms of the consistencies, interviewees in all four case studies emphasised the environmental aspect of social performance, including

(a) environmental sustainability (Case A)
(b) recycling and reduction in energy consumption (Case B)
(c) reduced paper usage, reduction in energy usage, encouragement of homeworking, accredited training courses in environmental management for its corporate customers and environmental consultancy reviews (Case C)
(d) reduction in energy consumption, encouragement of use of public transport and car sharing, reduced paper usage and recycling (Case D).

In all four case studies interviewees also stressed community involvement, including

(a) the development of disadvantaged communities in developing countries into mainstream suppliers and all employees participating in community projects (Case A)
(b) community (particularly local community) involvement by employees, charitable donations in cash and kind, and educational liaison including employees visiting schools, courses for school pupils and teacher placements (Case B)
(c) community support including sponsorship (Case C)
(d) community involvement by employees and charitable donations (Case D).

Interviewees in all four case studies considered the treatment of employees as part of the organisation's social performance, including

(a) treating employees right', employee surveys and employee dialogue group (Case A)
(b) staff morale, annual employee opinion survey and employee reverse feedback programme, i.e. feedback on managers by their subordinates (Case B)

(c) group working and how each employees job fits into the rest of their life (Case C)

(d) employee commitment, employee satisfaction and question- naire survey of employees (Case D).

In all four case studies interviewees mentioned suppliers when dis- cussing the meaning of social performance, including

(a) ethical trading policy (including paying suppliers on time), social performance of suppliers (including audits of major sup- pliers by an independent third party) and supply chain integrity programme (Case A)

(b) paying suppliers on time and developing long-term relation- ships with suppliers (Case B)

(c) supply chain strategy including social performance of suppliers and paying suppliers on time (Case C)

(d) suppliers'environmental impact, how suppliers treat their own employees, how suppliers treat their own suppliers and paying suppliers promptly (Case D).

Externally reported social performance measures and decision-making

In three of the case studies (namely A, B and C) many of the inter- viewees had little knowledge of the specific externally reported social performance measures. The interviewees in Cases A, B and C generally ignored or even did not know about the externally reported social performance measures. One reason for this seemed to be because a separate, self-contained unit (divorced from the operational managers and management accountants in the organisa- tion) reported these social performance measures.

Generally, the externally reported social performance measures did not come from the internal management reporting system but were collected as a one-off exercise by this self-contained unit. As a result, very often there was no internal management reporting, monitoring or management of such externally reported social per- formance measures. Most interviewees viewed the external social report of their organisation as a very separate event that did not impact on their job or decision-making. The general view emerging from the interviewees in the case studies was that the main purpose of externally reported social performance measures was for public relations. Such external reporting was aimed not only at shareholders but also at the community and customers.

The basic finding, therefore, is that the externally reported social performance measures had very little *direct* influence on managerial decision-making in Cases A, B and C. Even in Case D where interviewees were more aware of the externally reported social performance measures, the basic finding from the interviews was that *D*'s social accountability programme had not yet permeated into daily decision-making. Perhaps as organisations adopt a comprehensive framework for reporting, such as AA 1000 (published by the Institute of Social and Ethical AccountAbility in 1999), the gap between externally reported social performance measures and internally reported social performance measures may diminish. However, a significant finding was that despite this gap, managers placed great emphasis on social issues in decision-making. Indeed, in Cases A, B and C the extent to which social values influenced decisions and the culture of the organisation far exceeded the externally reported social performance.

Hence, although the externally reported social performance measures had little direct influence on managerial decision-making, in all four cases the social values and culture of each organisation did influence managerial decision-making, including the following examples:

1. Case A had the following concerns:
   (a) for company's effect on society
   (b) for individuals
   (c) for environment
   that were partially incorporated in the formal managerial controls. However, *A*'s values and culture (via individual employees' self-control and informal group control) influenced individual decisions such as use of green diesel (in spite of extra costs), reduction in use of energy, design of *A*'s products and packaging, use of refillable containers and use of recycled materials.
2. In Case B, the formal mission statement did state that it would be an 'ethical company', but its values and culture translated this into organisational values such as:
   (a) integrity
   (b) valuing staff
   (c) management by fact
   (d) trustworthy and caring organisation.

B's values and culture influenced decisions such as local community involvement, educational liaison work by employees, developing long-term relationships with suppliers and its emphasis on the importance of staff morale.

3. In Case C, its values and culture influenced managerial decision-making. As illustration, *C*

   (a) did not deal with companies whose ethics and values did not match *C*'s brand values of integrity and trust

   (b) required its potential suppliers to include a statement of their environmental policy in the tender process

   (c) was working to overcome social exclusion by finding ways to offer insurance to those previously excluded

   (d) was encouraging homeworking and remote vehicle inspections to reduce car travel.

4. In Case D where interviewees were more aware of the externally reported social performance measures, the interviewees still considered the culture and values of the organisation to be a very important influence on managerial decision-making. For example, *D* now integrated environmental considerations into decisions about both its own properties and its investment properties. Similarly, the investment in a new electronic document management system was justified on grounds that included both less use of paper and also less use of energy.

Internally and externally reported social performance measures

A major objective of this research project was to try to determine the degree to which internally and externally reported social performance measures were consistent. This was the reason for selecting four organisations at the leading edge of external social reporting. The overall finding was that the internally reported social performance measures were much less developed than the externally reported social performance measures. Indeed, in Cases A, B and C there were relatively few internally reported social performance measures, and only in Case D were the internally reported social performance measures linked to those published in the social report. Conversely, in Cases A, B and C, initiatives directed towards social values significantly exceeded those that were reported to external parties. A summary of the internally reported social performance measures follows on a case by case basis.

Case A

In Case A the internally reported social performance measures were much less developed than the performance measures in the published social report. Case A did report a number of measures related to employees such as:

1. absenteeism
2. sickness rate
3. appraisal completion rate
4. employee satisfaction rate
5. percentage of employees involved in community projects.

Case A also reported internally a large range of performance measures related to its suppliers such as:

1. minimum age for employees
2. employees have proper written contracts
3. factories have proper licences from the government
4. impact on the environment.

However, *A* had no internally reported social performance measures in relation to its community involvement or environmental impact.

Case B

Case B did have more extensive internal reporting of social performance measures than Case A and used a performance measurement scorecard covering

1. customer satisfaction
2. people satisfaction
3. impact on society
4. financial results.

The people satisfaction measures included

1. staff morale index
2. employees'perceptions of job security

3. index of job offering feeling of personal accomplishment
4. employees'perceptions of competitiveness of salary.

The impact-on-society measures included

1. press coverage
2. extent to which *B* enforces corporate governance in companies where *B* is a shareholder
3. external recognition awards
4. community investment measures including
    (a) number of staff secondments
    (b) charitable amount raised by staff
    (c) number of employee hours per week on community projects.

However, *B* had no internally reported social performance measures in relation to its environment impact or its suppliers.

Case C

Case C was similar to Case B in that it used a balanced scorecard approach with internally reported performance measures covering employees and *C*'s impact on the environment. The employee measures included

1. absenteeism rate
2. staff retention rate
3. staff enthusiasm index
4. development of teamwork
5. level of employees'skill base.

The environmental measures included

1. use of paper
2. number of miles travelled by car
3. energy consumption.

However, *C* had no internally reported social performance measures in relation to its community involvement or its suppliers.

Case D

In Cases A, B and C there were no links between the internally and externally reported social performance measures. In contrast, in

Case D the internally reported social performance measures were explicitly linked to the published measures. D's social accountability programme had influenced its internal performance measurement system that used key performance indicators. D had a very detailed system with more than 100 objectives covering community, customers, employees, environment, investees and others. To give a flavour of the internally reported social performance measures the 41 environmental measures included the following measures reported against targets:

1. data on CO_2 emissions
2. environmental criteria for selection of suppliers
3. quantities of recycled materials in purchased products
4. environmental impact of D's company car scheme
5. data on water use
6. volume of waste produced and sent to landfill
7. volume of waste recycled.

Social information needs of managers

In Cases A, B and C managers generally considered that they received too little social information and, in particular, both accountants and managers agreed that there were too few social performance measures reported internally. In Case A there were few explicit links between the social aspects of its mission statement and its internal performance measurement system. Both accountants and managers in A accepted the need to report internally more social information. Interviewees agreed that A reported internally a reasonable amount of social information about its suppliers and to a lesser extent, its employees. However, interviewees mentioned the following areas where more social information could be reported internally:

1. community involvement such as percentage of staff involved and also numbers involved in initiatives such as work experience, teacher placements and school visits
2. survey results such as quality of feedback in relation to community involvement
3. environmental impact such as amount of waste produced and percentage recycled.

Similarly in Case B there was a gap between the externally reported social objectives and the internally reported social information. Interviewees would have liked more information, particularly about *B's* environmental performance so that they could act to improve it. *B* was beginning to explore the costs and values of its community involvement and managers agreed that such information might help them to improve the overall benefit of *B's* community involvement to society. In addition managers in *B* would be interested to know the views of the recipients of *B's* community involvement.

In Case C interviewees highlighted a gap between the social aspects of its mission statement and its internal performance measurement system. *C's* interviewees accepted that some social information was reported about employees and the environment but suggested that more information could be reported internally about the social performance of *C's* suppliers and also about *C's* community involvement. Again interviewees suggested both input measures (such as the number of employees involved and the hours spent on community projects) and output or outcome measures (such as the effects of *C's* community involvement on society – for example, feedback from those affected).

In contrast to Cases A, B and C, Case D did have explicit links between its externally and internally reported social performance measures. The interviewees in D liked its comprehensive internal reporting of social performance measures. However, even with this very detailed social performance measurement system, many interviewees in *D* considered that the system had too much emphasis on input measures and too little on outcome measures. For example, some interviewees mentioned that *D* had not yet begun a dialogue with communities about the effects of *D's* community involvement.

Social performance measures and performance evaluation system

At present in all four cases, social performance is not part of the formal performance evaluation and remuneration system. Almost all the interviewees in the four cases recognised that this was a weakness. Some interviewees argued that if social performance is part of the organisation's mission statement and is an important aspect of its business, then both the performance evaluation and remuneration systems for individuals needed to take a contribution to the organisation's social performance explicitly into account. Only *A* and *D* of the four organisations were considering changing their performance evaluation system to take the social performance aspect explicitly into account. Furthermore, neither *A* nor *D* were yet at the stage of considering changing their remuneration system to include an individual's contribution to the organisation's social performance.

Conclusions

Reasons for emphasis on social performance

In each of the four case studies, the interviewees were asked why they thought that their particular organisation was concerned about its own social performance. The majority of the replies can be summarised as follows:

1. each organisation wished to be an ethical organisation respected for its environmental and social performance and its ethical behaviour
2. such an ethical, environmental and social image was considered 'good for business' and, although there might be increased costs for the organisation in the short run, the interviewees believed that the long-term effect was positive on the bottom line of the organisation.

Some of the interviewees had joined that particular organisation at least partly because of its good social image and its future social performance was very important for such individuals. However, even these individuals accepted that the long-term business case (and the effect on the bottom line)'for the social performance of the organisation was very important. It was not simply social performance for its own sake but rather meeting society's expectations and therefore improving their organisations' own reputation. Indeed, each of the four organisations to a greater or lesser extent took advantage of its social image in its marketing. Most of the interviewees in all four organisations believed that the social image of the organisation was very important for several of the stakeholder groups including their customers.

Views of accountants and managers

Nine accountants and forty-one managers were interviewed in the four case studies. Obviously this is a relatively small number of accountants but no major differences were found between the views of accountants and managers. For example, both accountants and managers agreed that managers needed more social information and that there should be explicit links between the externally and internally reported social performance measures.

Three differences did emerge in relation to the managers in the four cases. First, and not surprisingly, functional managers tended to give more emphasis to their particular function in relation to social performance. For example, a Human Relations Manager would give particular emphasis to the employee aspect of social performance and a Purchasing Manager would stress the importance of suppliers to social performance. Secondly, more senior managers tended to suggest a wider range of stakeholder groups than lower level managers. Thirdly, lower level managers generally asked for more detailed social performance information than more senior managers.

Stakeholders

The stakeholder groups identified by the interviewees in all four organisations were remarkably similar, namely

- Communities (term used by most interviewees rather than society)
- Customers
- Employees
- Environment
- Shareholders (where applicable)
- Suppliers.

A and *D* also included investees (i.e. companies in which *A* and *D* invested). Although the six stakeholder groups were very similar for all four organisations, the priority given to different stakeholder groups varied between the four organisations.

Although the stakeholder approach was adopted by all four organisations, it cannot be assumed that equal weight was given to different stakeholder groups or even that the same ranking was given to stakeholder groups. This suggests that it is important to discover for each organisation its own ranking of stakeholder groups. This is significant because most interviewees accepted that at times there would be conflicts and trade-offs between different stakeholder groups in relation to social performance.

All four organisations conducted surveys of at least some of their stakeholder groups. The most common surveys were of customers and employees. Some organisations tried to conduct some form of dialogue with other stakeholder groups such as communities and suppliers. All four organisations emphasised communities and the environment in relation to their social performance. However, again the degree of emphasis on communities and the environment varied between the four organisations. In summary, the general stakeholder approach was important for all four organisations in relation to their social performance, but the priority given to different stakeholder groups varied between the four organisations.

Decision-making

There were a number of examples from each of the four organisations where the social values of the organisation had influenced managerial decision-making. However, almost all the interviewees in Cases A, B and C considered that the externally reported social performance measures had little direct influence on managerial decision-making. *A* was perhaps the most extreme of the four cases where it published many social performance measures but the general view of the interviewees could be summarised by the following quote from an interviewee:

> My perspective is that in the past in this company, social reporting was an event unto itself, and it was important to get all this information out there in voluminous detail but in reality it had very little to do with the business at all.

In Cases A, B and C this lack of direct influence of the externally reported social performance measures on managerial decision-making was more than compensated by the influence of each organisation's culture and social values on its decision-making. These influences had such an impact that social value-based decisions extended well beyond the detail in the external social performance reports. Details of each of the four organisations'culture and social values are discussed in Chapter 7 together with their influence on decision-making.

All four organisations had decided that community involvement was a good idea. This community involvement took different forms such as staff working on local community projects, sponsorship of community projects and helping underdeveloped communities to become suppliers. However, generally there was a change of emphasis from giving money to supporting In kind'– usually in the form of staff time. In this way community involvement not only helped the community involved but also the organisation itself benefited in the form of staff development and often in the form of team building. As one interviewee suggested:

> Community involvement is much more self-interested than charitable giving.

However, the general view was that both the communities and the organisations themselves gained more from community involvement than from simply cash donations.

Internal performance measures

Generally the internally reported social performance measures were underdeveloped relative to the externally reported social performance measures. There were very few explicit links between the externally and internally reported social performance measures (with the exception of one case, namely *D*). Furthermore, the links between either the externally or internally reported social performance measures and the evaluation system for managers were almost non-existent in all four cases. In summary, the external reporting of social performance measures did not mean that these same measures were applied internally and did not mean that there was a formal system for monitoring and managing social performance.

Nevertheless, internal social performance measures did exist, such as in relation to:

◆ Communities (such as percentage of employees participating in community projects, number of employee hours per week on community projects, level of community trade and level of community investment)
◆ Customers (such as customer satisfaction measure)
◆ Employees (such as employee satisfaction index, employee retention rate, employees' perceptions of job security and job offering a feeling of personal accomplishment)
◆ Environment (such as energy usage, use of water, volume of waste produced, volume of waste recycled, employees'car travel and use of paper)
◆ Suppliers (such as minimum age for employees, factories have proper licences from the government and impact on the environment).

Some of these internal social performance measures were also benchmarked against the performance of other organisations.

Most of the interviewees accepted that their organisation needed to develop better internal social performance measures to provide higher quality information for managers so that they could improve the management of their organisations social performance. There was also general agreement among the interviewees that the internal social performance measures that did exist concentrated too much on input measures and neglected output or outcome measures. Interviewees attributed the relative underdevelopment of internal social performance measures in Cases A, B and C to two main reasons:

1. The external social performance reporting of the organisation was a separate event disconnected from the internal management of the organisation.
2. The values and culture of the organisation were as important as the current internal social performance measures in influencing the actual social performance of the organisation.

However, in relation to the above second point, the interviewees considered that the current, internally reported social perform-ance measures could be further developed and new measures introduced. Most interviewees believed that such development and expansion of the internal social performance measures would help managers to act to improve the organisations social performance.

Social values and controls

In all four cases interviewees considered the social values and culture of the organisation to be important to the social performance of the organisation. All four organisations had their explicit values such as effect on society, concern for individual, concern for environment, concern about policies of suppliers, management by fact, valuing staff, ethical behaviour, trust and integrity. In A the Values Group played an important role with their monthly report to the Executive Committee and in D the Social Values Working Group with its 60 facilitators influenced aspects such as equal opportunities and community involvement.

There was also a willingness in all four cases to transmit their values to others. For example, *A* and *C* passed on their values to their suppliers. *B* and *D* had ethical investment funds with explicit social values. *D* also transmitted its environmental values to tenants in their buildings. *C* did not deal with corporate customers whose ethics and values did not match its brand values of integrity and trust.

Just as each of the four organisations had different values, so the interviewees in each of the four organisations had a slightly different interpretation of what is meant by social performance. Such differences were usually related to the different priorities given to the various stakeholder groups. However, one similarity between the four organisations was the importance of self-control and informal group control in relation to social performance. Most interviewees considered the current formal management controls (such as internal performance measures and budgets) to be less important than the informal controls (such as group control and culture) in terms of their influence on the organisations' social performance. However, again this was at least partly because of the relative underdevelopment of the internally reported social performance measures.

How did such informal controls arise? In all four organisations (but particularly in *A* and *B*), a great deal of effort was put into the employee recruitment and induction processes. Indeed in *A* and *B* the interviewees suggested that job applicants were at least partially influenced by a desire to work in socially and ethically oriented' organisations. There was evidence that job applicants were rejected because they had values incompatible with those of the organisation. After a very thorough recruitment process, all four organisations also had an extensive induction process that included an emphasis on the organisations' values. For example, new recruits to *A* spent some time working on a community project during their induction period. Undoubtedly the most important formal control in relation to social performance in each of the four organisations was the recruitment and induction process.

Following this recruitment and induction process, each of the four organisations relied mainly on the self-control of individual employees and informal group control in relation to social performance. The interviewees considered that the values and culture of each organisation rather than the current internal performance measurement system drove decision-making and influenced the organisation's interaction with society. Nevertheless, in their feedback on our written Case Studies A, B and C accepted that better formal internal reporting of its own social performance would probably help managers to take decisions to improve the organisation's social performance. Indeed, in their feedback, Cases A, B and C all stated that they were planning to develop explicit links between their externally and internally reported social performance measures.

Findings in relation to literature

Some of the findings from this research project are in agreement with previous findings or statements in the literature but some of our findings are contrary to previous research findings. For example, the findings from this project support the emphasis given to stakeholders in the social reporting literature (see, for example, Clarkson, 1995; Griffin and Mahon, 1997; Greening and Turban, 2000). Similarly, this project's findings support the importance of culture and values in the social performance area (see, for example, Falkenberg and Herremans, 1995; Adams, 1999 in the ethical area). Similar to the finding of Adams (1999) that few people are involved in compiling the corporate report on ethical issues, so one finding of this project is that a small, separate unit within each organisation prepared the external social report and this unit was very much divorced from the rest of the organisation.

In contrast to the above, some findings from this project did not support previous findings or statements in the literature. For example, research studies (such as Burns *et al.*, 1996) found that managers were influenced by external reporting but, in Cases A, B and C, managers were not directly influenced by external social reporting. Starovic (2002, p. 12) suggested that 'reporting should be supported by a robust internal architecture for measuring performance' but in Cases A, B and C this was not the case. A possible reason for the failure of externally reported social performance measures to be reflected in the internal social measures can be found in Gray (2000, p. 262) who has suggested that the accounting profession is standing back and letting inexperienced individuals and organisations take over and define the accounting and audit agendas in social and environmental accounting.

Developing Internal Social Performance Information Systems (ISPIS)

The findings of this research project suggest a number of recommendations for management accountants to consider if they wish to implement internal social performance reporting. These recommendations can be summarised as follows:

1. Have an implementation team involving a management accountant and managers but probably led by a manager so that it is seen as a management rather than an accounting-led approach.
2. Consult managers about the social information and social performance measures that they need to help them to improve the organisation's social performance.
3. (a) If your organisation already has an external social report, develop explicit links between the externally and internally reported social performance measures.

   (b) If your organisation does not have an external social report, consider developing first internal social performance measures and reports and then, if your organisation wishes, an external social report can be developed from the social performance measures used internally.
4. Develop logical links between your organisation's mission statement/objectives and your internally reported social performance measures.
5. Choose the stakeholder groups for your particular organisation and also try to rank these groups in order of priority and identify any potential conflicts between these stakeholder groups.
6. Develop internal social performance measures for each of your organisation's stakeholder groups.
7. Check that the internally reported social performance measures include both input and outcome measures. For example, for community involvement, input measures might include

(a) number of employees participating in community involvement

(b) total employee hours per week spent on community involvement

(c) total costs of community involvement

and outcome measures might include

(a) feedback from those affected by such community involvement

(b) value of community involvement.

8. Develop a formal system for internal monitoring and management of social performance.

9. Develop explicit links between managerial evaluation (and remuneration) and contribution to organisation's social performance.

10. The internally reported social performance measures are important but so are the organisation's culture and social values that affect social performance – for example, through informal group control and employee self-control.

Overview

External reporting of social performance measures in these four case studies did not mean that the same measures were used internally. Furthermore, external social reporting did not imply that there was necessarily a formal system of internal monitoring or management of social performance. However, a lack of a formal system of internal social performance measurement did not mean that an organisation did not care about social performance. In all four organisations a very thorough recruitment and induction process, coupled with the social values of the organisation, led to informal group control and self-control influencing each of the four organisations'social performance.

The four case studies also revealed many examples of the social values of each organisation affecting its decision-making. The interviewees identified very similar stakeholder groups in each organisation (communities, customers, employees, environment, shareholders and suppliers) but the priority ranking for each of these stakeholder groups varied among the four organisations. This meant that the interviewees in each of the four organisations had slightly different views on what is meant by social performance.

Many interviewees said without any prompting that their organisation needed to improve the social information reported to managers. The interviewees suggested the following areas where improvements could be made so that managers could better manage an organisation's social performance:

1. better links between external and internal social performance measures
2. more social performance outcome or output (as distinct from input) measures
3. better internal reporting of social performance
4. improved means of ranking the concerns of different stakeholders
5. better formal controls in relation to social performance
6. explicit links between managerial evaluation (and remuneration) and an organisation's social performance.

However, even with the above improvements to the formal systems in relation to social performance, the informal systems (such as group control and self-control) will remain very important. These four case studies suggest that the values and culture of an organisation are critical factors affecting its social performance. Research into external social reporting is important but so is research into management information and social performance and, in particular, into Internal Social Performance Information Systems (ISPIS). In the final analysis it is the strategic and operating decisions of managers and other employees that determine the social performance of an organisation.

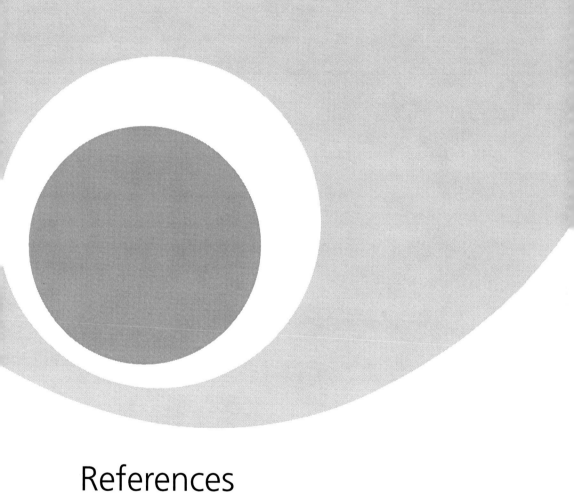

References

Adams, C. (1999), *The Nature and Processes of Corporate Reporting on Ethical Issues*, Chartered Institute of Management Accountants, London.

Adams, C., Hill, W. and Roberts, C. (1995), *Environmental, Employee and Ethical Reporting in Europe*, Association of Chartered Certified Accountants, London.

Adams, C.A., Hill, W.Y. and Roberts, C.B. (1998), Corporate Social Reporting Practices in Western Europe: Legitimating Corporate Behaviour, *The British Accounting Review*, Vol. 30, No. 1, pp. 1–21.

Bebbington, J. and Thompson, I. (1996), *Business Concepts of Sustainability and the Implications for Accountancy*, Association of Chartered Certified Accountants, London.

Bennett, M. and James, P. (1998), *The Green Bottom Line: Environmental Accounting for Management*, Greenleaf, Sheffield.

Bennett, M. and James, P. (1999), *Sustainable Measures: Evaluation and Reporting of Environmental and Social Performance*, Greenleaf, Sheffield.

Berle, A.A. and Means, G.C. (1932), *The Modern Corporation and Private Property*, Macmillan, New York.

Bowen, H.R. (1953), *Social Responsibilities of the Businessman*, Harper & Row, New York.

Burns, J., Joseph, N., Lewis, L., Scapens, R., Southworth, A. and Turley, S. (1996), *External Reporting and Management Decisions: A Study of Their Interrelationship in UK Companies*, Chartered Institute of Management Accountants, London.

Burritt, R.L. (1998), Cost Allocation: An Active Tool for Environmental Management Accounting? in Bennett, M. and James, P. *The Green Bottom Line*, Greenleaf, Sheffield, pp. 152–163.

Carroll, A.B. (1979), A Three-Dimensional Conceptual Model of Corporate Social Performance, *Academy of Management Review*, Vol. 4, No. 4, pp. 497–505.

Chartered Institute of Management Accountants (1997), *Environmental Management: The Role of the Management Accountant*, CIMA, London.

Clarkson, M.B.E. (1995), A Stakeholder Framework for Analyzing and Evaluating Corporate Social Performance, *Academy of Management Review*, Vol. 20, No. 1, pp. 92–117.

Dey, C. (1999), *Social Accounting and Accountability*, Doctoral Dissertation, University of Dundee.

Dey, C., Evans, R. and Gray, R.H. (1995), Towards Social Information and Bookkeeping: A Note on Developing the Mechanisms for Social Accounting and Audit, *Journal of Applied Accounting Research*, Vol. 2, No. 3, pp. 33–63.

Donaldson, T. and Preston, L.E. (1995), The Stakeholder Theory of the Corporation: Concepts, Evidence and Implications, *Academy of Management Review*, Vol. 20, No. 1, pp. 65–91.

Epstein, M.J. and Roy, M.J. (1998), Integrating Environmental Impacts into Capital Investment Decisions, in Bennett, M. and James, P. *The Green Bottom Line*, Greenleaf, Sheffield, pp. 115–128.

Estes, R. (1992), Social Accounting Past and Future: Should the Profession Lead, Follow or Just Get Out of the Way, *Advances in Management Accounting*, Vol. 1, pp. 97–108.

Falkenberg, L. and Herremans, I. (1995), Ethical Behaviour in Organisations: Directed by the Formal or Informal Systems, *Journal of Business Ethics*, Vol. 14, No. 2, pp. 133–157.

Frederick, W.C. (1994), From CSR1 to CSR2: The Maturing of Business and Society Thought, *Business and Society*, Vol. 33, No. 2, pp. 150–164.

Gatewood, R.D. and Carroll, A. (1991), Assessment of Ethical Performance of Organization Members: A Conceptual Framework, *Academy of Management Review*, Vol. 16, No. 4, pp. 667–690.

Gonella, C., Pilling, A. and Zadek, S. (1998), *Making Values Count: Contemporary Experience in Social and Ethical Accounting, Auditing and Reporting*, Certified Accountants Educational Trust, London.

Gray, R.H. (2000), Current Developments and Trends in Social and Environmental Auditing, Reporting and Attestation: A Review and Comment, *International Journal of Auditing*, Vol. 4, No. 3, pp. 247–268.

Gray, R.H., Owen, D.L. and Maunders, K.T. (1988), Corporate Social Reporting: Emerging Trends in Accountability and the Social Contract, *Accounting, Auditing and Accountability Journal*, Vol. 1, No. 1, pp. 6–20.

Gray, R.H., Owen, D.L. and Maunders, K.T. (1991), Accountability, Corporate Social Reporting and the Social Contract, *Accounting, Auditing and Accountability Journal*, Vol. 4, No. 1, pp. 36–50.

Gray, R.H., Kouhy, R. and Lavers, S. (1995), Corporate Social and Environmental Reporting: A Review of the Literature and a Longitudinal Study of UK Disclosure, *Accounting, Auditing and Accountability Journal*, Vol. 8, No. 2, pp. 417–447.

Gray, R.H., Dey, C., Owen, D., Evans, R. and Zadek, S. (1997), Struggling with the Praxis of Social Accounting: Stakeholders, Accountability, Audits and Procedures, *Accounting, Auditing and Accountability Journal*, Vol. 10, No. 3, pp. 325–364.

Greening, D.W. and Turban, D.B. (2000), Corporate Social Performance as a Competitive Advantage in Attracting a Quality Workforce, *Business and Society*, Vol. 39, No. 3, pp. 254–280.

Griffin, J.J. and Mahon, J.F. (1997), The Corporate Social Performance and Corporate Financial Performance Debate: Twenty-five Years of Incomparable Research, *Business and Society*, Vol. 36, No. 1, pp. 5–31.

Harte, G. and Owen, D.L. (1991), Environmental Disclosure in Annual Reports of British Companies: A Research Note, *Accounting, Auditing and Accountability Journal*, Vol. 4, No. 3, pp. 51–61.

Hayward, C. (2002), How to be Good, *Financial Management*, October, p. 14.

Husted, B.W. (2000), A Contingency Theory of Corporate Social Performance, *Business and Society*, Vol. 39, No. 1, pp. 24–48.

King, A. (2002), How to Get Started in Corporate Social Responsibility, *Financial Management*, October, p. 5.

Lehman, G. (1999), Disclosing New Worlds: A Role for Social and Environmental Accounting and Auditing, *Accounting Organizations and Society*, Vol. 24, No. 1, pp. 217–241.

Matthews, M.R. (1997), Twenty Five Years of Social and Environmental Accounting Research: Is There a Silver Jubilee to Celebrate, *Accounting, Auditing and Accountability Journal*, Vol. 10, No. 4, pp. 481–531.

McIntosh, M., Leipziger, D., Jones, K. and Coleman, G. (1998), *Corporate Citizenship: Successful Strategies for Responsible Companies*, Financial Times, London.

Mitchell, R., Agle, B. and Wood, D. (1997), Toward a Theory of Stakeholder Identification and Salience: Defining the Principle of Who and What Really Counts, *Academy of Management Review*, Vol. 22, No. 4, pp. 853–886.

ODwyer, B. (2001), The Legitimacy of Accountants' Participation in Social and Ethical Accounting, Auditing and Reporting, *Business Ethics: A European Review*, Vol. 10, No. 1, pp. 27–39.

Owen, D.L., Gray, R.H. and Adams, R. (1997), *Corporate Environmental Disclosure: Encouraging Trends*, Association of Chartered Certified Accountants, London.

Owen, D.L., Swift, T.A., Humphrey, C. and Bowerman, M. (2000), The New Social Audits: Accountability, Managerial Capture or the Agenda Champions, *European Accounting Review*, Vol. 9, No. 1, pp. 81–98.

Robin, D.P. and Reidenbach, R.E. (1987), Social Responsibility, Ethics and Marketing Strategy: Closing the Gaps Between Concept and Application, *Journal of Marketing*, Vol. 51, pp. 44–58.

Rose, J. (2003), Corporate Social Responsibility: The Importance of Being Earnest, *The Age* (a Melbourne newspaper), 6 January 2003, p. 5.

Sethi, S.P. (1995), Introduction to AMR's Special Topic Forum on Shifting Paradigms: Societal Expectations and Corporate Performance, *Academy of Management Review*, Vol. 20, No. 1, pp. 18–21.

Sharfman, M.P., Pinkston, T.S. and Sigerstad, T.D. (2000), The Effects of Managerial Values on Social Issues Evaluation: An Empirical Examination, *Business and Society*, Vol. 39, No. 2, pp. 144–182.

Singhapakdi, A., Salyachivin, S., Virakul, V. and Veerangkur, V. (2000), Some Important Factors Underlying Ethical Decision Making of Managers in Thailand, *Journal of Business Ethics*, Vol. 27, No. 4, pp. 271–284.

Soutar, G., McNeil, M. and Molster, C. (1994), The Impact of the Work Environment on Ethical Decision Making: Some Australian Evidence, *Journal of Business Ethics*, Vol. 13, No. 5, pp. 327–340.

Starovic, D. (2002), Green Signals Go', *Financial Management*, October, p. 12.

Strauss, A. and Corbin, J. (1998), *Basics of Qualitative Research: Techniques and Procedures for Developing Grounded Theory*, Sage, Thousand Oaks.

Swanson, D.L. (1995), Addressing a Theoretical Problem by Re-orienting the Corporate Social Performance Model, *Academy of Management Review*, Vol. 20, No. 1, pp. 43–64.

United Nations (2000), *Environmental Management Accounting Procedures and Principles*, U.N. Division for Sustainable Development, New York.

Verbeke, W., Ouwerkerk, C. and Peelen, E. (1996), Exploring the Contextual and Individual Factors on Ethical Decision Making of Sales People, *Journal of Business Ethics*, Vol. 15, No. 11, pp. 1175–1187.

Votaw, D. (1972), Genius Becomes Rare, in Votaw, D. and Sethi, S.P. (eds), *The Corporate Dilemma*, Prentice-Hall, Englewood Cliffs.

Wartick, S.L. and Cochran, P.L. (1985), The Evolution of the Corporate Social Performance Model, *Academy of Management Review*, Vol. 10, No. 4, pp. 758–769.

Wood, D.J. (1991), Corporate Social Performance Revisited, *Academy of Management Journal*, Vol. 16, No. 4, pp. 691–718.

Woodward, D., Edwards, P. and Birkin, F. (2001), Some Evidence on Executives' Views of Corporate Social Responsibility, *British Accounting Review*, Vol. 33, No. 1, September, pp. 357–397.

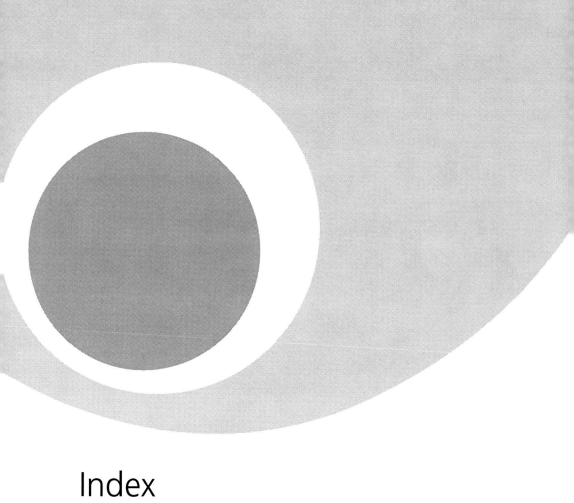

Index